"Thought provoking! A breakthrough in defining the convergence of new technology and the spiritual evolution of our time."

~ Steve Brass, Founder and President of Link to Life Seminars Inc. and Author of Fearless Living

"An Exciting work that reveals hot-button opportunities that can be turned into profits in the networked economy."

~ James Thomson, President, Bayview International Insurance Brokers Inc.

"A fascinating and insightful look at how to use a principle-centered approach for greater harmony and success in your business and personal life."

~ Kenneth Drabble, Vice President, Senior Financial Advisor, Equion Securities Canada Limited

"A book that uncovers trends and coming changes for our key institutions, business, government, and family."

~ Jeff Dinsmore, President, Can Am Special Risk Management

63 Trends to Understanding the Future

Business & Social
Trendz

Profiting with Spiritual Economics

G.ROBERT SWITZER

Abbeyfield Publishers
2000 Toronto, Ontario

Canadian Cataloguing in Publication Data
Switzer, G. Robert (George Robert)

Business & Social Trendz:
profiting with spiritual economics

ISBN 1-894584-02-3
1. Business / inspirational / self-help. I. Title.

HF5387.S94 2000   174'.4   C00-930927-6

Editor ~ Shelly Drayton

Project management ~
The Abbeyfield Companies Ltd.

Cover and textual design ~ Karen Petherick
Cover illustration ~ Michael Petherick

Back cover photo ~ Faizal Sharif

Digital Imagery® copyright 1999 PhotoDisk, Inc.

Dedicated to my Spiritual Guide
the Mahanta

To John

Best Wishes with your
hospice work

Bob
Nov 14 2006

A C K N O W L E D G E M E N T S

With heartfelt thanks
to Harold,
Andrea, Kay, Bill, Karen, Shelley
Marina, Shirley, Janice and Eitan,

for your advice and encouragement.

TABLE OF CONTENTS

The Macro Trend

THERE IS A HUGE SHIFT GAINING MOMENTUM IN THE WORLD AND IT WILL LEAD TO MANY CHANGES. At its most basic level, this book is an explanation of the various factors that are combining to change your world and mine. In that sense, it could be called a leader's guide to change in the new millennium because as leaders, of course, we want to be successful. And, if you can see and understand the coming changes, you will be able to move with them in order to profit and lead others with a new sense of vision.

Of course, the changes most of us are aware of, to some extent or another, are the technological changes that are everywhere apparent. Today, the trend of technological convergence, predicted in the 80's, is playing out before our eyes. No longer do computer companies such as Hewlett Packard see themselves as computer manufacturing companies, nor does AOL (after its merger with Time Warner) see itself simply as a network to users, and cable companies are no longer defining themselves as being in the transmission and delivery of entertainment. The convergence of technologies (hardware, software and communications) is now the focus of these redefined technologies companies. They deliver business and consumer capabilities and solutions. This convergence is, in many ways, a sign of things to come.

I believe we are actually experiencing a technological revolution as we move to a society that is totally supported by technology. In 20 years, the world will be significantly changed as we adopt new enabling systems, and the children of the boomers, the "eco" generation, will be the drivers of the new technology and its incorporation into our lives. These technological advances and changes will absolutely change the way that we do business. There is, however, another dimension to this transition: the human dimension. We will have to change in order to be able to use these coming gifts to society. Our ability to accept and foster this change to a technologically enabled world is crucial.

The human ability to accept and integrate a shift of this magnitude will require a new adaptability and flexibility on our part, if we are to take full advantage of the revolution to come in a way that will enrich our lives. In fact, we will have to change not only our view of ourselves and of our world, but how we interact with each other in order to successfully integrate the new technologies into our lives. And this brings us to another major change that is taking place in our society today.

Concurrent with the technological changes, there is a shift in values taking place as we discover that we want to be more than simply survivors or moneymakers in our lifetime. We, as a society, are starting to look inwardly for answers to life's deepest questions and we are discovering that there is a greater meaning to life, if we open ourselves to that possibility. In essence, we are becoming aware of our own spiritual nature and, as a society, we are moving towards being Spiritual-Values driven. This seed urge to discover our spiritual nature is buried deep within our hearts and is now emerging. In the optimum scenario, the technological changes will give us the ability and freedom to pursue this quest for personal growth.

This book, then, is about the coming technological changes and how we will adapt to them. But it is also about another hidden convergence—the convergence of technology with our spiritual unfoldment, as we shift to operating from a new set of values. This convergence is symbiotic in that each of these movements requires the other in order to lead us into the new society that we have the opportunity to create in the next 20 years. The new technological revolution is being enabled by our shift in values and, conversely, as we adopt the new technology, we are being given the opportunity to shift our values and grow as a society and as individuals.

And so, ultimately, this book is about helping you understand the convergence of Universal/Spiritual Values with the effects of the new technology, and the resulting new consciousness. These values include trust, honesty, respect, freedom, caring, forgiveness, listening, harmony, giving and many more. This writing assumes that you have some sensitivity to the concept that you are connected to the universe as a whole, and that you understand that you are here to do much more than to just get up in the morning, go to work, come home, relax, play, go to sleep and then get up and repeat the cycle again. For most people, however, life is like this until they are driven to realize that there must be more. And there is more, much more.

This book is about helping you understand the world from a spiritual perspective. It has been created as a bridge for those who know there is more to life and want to understand what is happening to the world. More than that, however, it is about helping you to order your life *and the life of your corporation* around these Spiritual Values, because by doing so you will be working with the flow of change, and you and your corporation will grow in ways you cannot possibly imagine. Some organizations are already there today, while others are still stuck in the industrial age.

The following chapters outline the qualities and values that are emerging and how to develop these to revitalize and re-energize organizations by re-energizing people. In these chapters, you will find over 60 trends identified, some of which overlap from chapter to chapter, just as these forces are interconnected in our lives. As you read, you will begin to understand how millions are redefining wealth to mean both a financial and a spiritual return. This shift will be the centerpiece of the changes in our society in the coming decade of transition.

This transition, now underway, is outlined in the first chapter, "The Millennium Shift." In the following chapters, I identify numerous business, personal, social and global trends and link them to the emerging Spiritual Values that are being rapidly adopted in our society. The chapters give some thoughts as to where these trends will lead and explore the basic and universal Spiritual Principles upon which these Spiritual Values are based. These underlying Spiritual Principles are the specific subject of the last chapter, for, when we first understand these Spiritual Principles that govern the universe, and then begin to order our lives around them, we can begin to live in true harmony with the universe.

Of course, a trend is simply a movement, action or tendency in or by a measurable and significant enough portion of our society that ultimately has the ability to affect the whole of society and its economic activity, to some extent. This is not to say that everyone will be involved in or affected by what is happening in the trends discussed in this book. In any trend, there is a hard core group that is leading, those who are half-heartedly following, and those who are actively resisting or are simply not choosing to be a part of the trend movement. This book deals with those who are an active part of this shift to an adoption of Spiritual Values and the resultant trends, and when I make the occasional generalization, it is to this group that I am referring. Still, these trends are general tendencies, not absolutes. Some are going to be stronger than others, and the strength of a trend, in the context of this book, is going to be determined by our degree of acceptance of these universal Spiritual Values as a prime motivator.

What is amazing to me is the discovery that there are so many human benefits that result from the adoption of Spiritual Values and which, at the same time, generate a greater wealth and profit for the individual or the corporation/organization. This book is therefore also about identifying opportunities for profit by understanding how the adoption of Spiritual Values will result in coming changes. For one thing is certain: These new Spiritual Values and underlying principles are now, and will continue to become, the hallmark of successful people and organizations in the years to come.

CHAPTER ONE

The Millennium Shift

We are living in exciting times. In fact, I believe we are living in the greatest transition mankind has ever experienced. Some see it as the greatest transfer of wealth, others call it the dawn of the communications age, but whatever you may call it, we are unquestionably in a period of great change that is shifting our world as we know it. As we leave the industrial age and enter a new era, tomorrow will definitely be different. But how will it be different? What will make it different? What are the forces causing this change and where will they lead us? We can gain an insight and better understanding of this change by looking at the underlying shift in values which is becoming increasingly evident in the world today.

Millions Are Asking, "Why Are We Here?"

There is a steadily surging interest in gaining a deeper understanding of who we are, why we are here, and what our relationship is to the whole of creation. We are awakening to the greater meaning life holds for us and the evidence of this awakening is all around us. Witness the Oprah Winfrey show with its regular focus on spiritual topics, the popularity of books like *The Celestine Prophecy,* movies such as "What Dreams May Come" and "The Green Mile," and television shows like "Touched by an Angel." Everywhere we look, the Spiritual is becoming an everyday topic of exploration and conversation. This interest is not being confined to the personal sphere either, but is also being reflected in the business arena. We have, for instance, seen two world conferences on "Spirituality in the Workplace" held in Toronto, Canada, in 1998 and 1999 and others in Boston, Santa Fe and Mexico. These examples are indicative of a significant shift in values which is taking place.

Our Values Are Shifting

Our societal values are changing as thousands of people search for and are finding greater truth by connecting with their "inner selves". Such values as kindness, charity, forgiveness, and humility are taking precedence and have begun to be referred to as Spiritual Values (see chapter 12 for a more comprehensive list of these values). These new Spiritual Values are evident and expressed in many of the major movements which began to garner mass involvement in the world in the closing years of the industrial age.

For example, millions of people are now expressing a heartfelt interest in the ecology of the world. For many, this is expressed through a genuine concern for and involvement in one or more specific cause, such as the various animal welfare movements, including causes to save the seals, whales, wolves or dolphins, or causes against animal cruelty or circuses to name a few. Land management issues are widely supported to prevent deforestation, protect the wetlands and halt urban sprawl. Air and water quality is a major hot button, and waste management has its proponents in the arenas of nuclear disposal, global warming and excessive packaging.

There is also a growing interest and mass participation in the wellness movement today, with an ever increasing number of people in Western society becoming involved in one or more of the various aspects of wellness. Alternative healing therapies, better nutrition and ingredient watchfulness, increasing demand for organic foods, and decreasing meat consumption and alcohol and tobacco usage are just a few examples of the shift in major values which is underway.

We are participating in programs of personal development on a large scale. The fitness industry is exploding, and both volunteerism and charitable giving are on the rise. Meanwhile, thousands of people are cashing out and making a transition to a simpler, quieter lifestyle at a slower pace, in a rejection of the pursuit of the almighty dollar. They are looking for a better balance in their lives. Millions of others are making best sellers of books such as "Conversations With God," and millions more are seeking and finding new Spiritual teachings which satisfy their desire for spiritual growth and understanding. Harold Klemp, the Spiritual leader of one such spiritual teaching, Eckankar, has authored over thirty books on the subject of helping people find their true inner selves, and the sale of such books is booming.

As millions of people express their new values in the areas of ecology, wellness and personal growth, they are also taking their first concerns and the corresponding values and transposing these to other areas of their life. As an example, what started out as a concern for the environment has now become a total lifestyle for millions of people. Spiritual Values are now a factor in the whole of their lives, including the realms of health, fitness, education, work and charity for these early adopters. Indeed, there is no separation as the new consciousness takes hold and we are seeing these values expressed in the whole of life. After all, how can one advocate honesty at work and be dishonest with friends? When the change is made in one area, it eventually affects the whole.

What all this says is that we are clearly changing. Life is taking on a deeper meaning for millions who are searching for truth. The adoption of new Spiritual Values is actually resulting in a change in consciousness which will accelerate as we move into the new decade.

Our Consciousness is Changing as We Reach Critical Mass

Our consciousness can actually be defined as our degree of awareness, understanding, and acceptance of who we are in relationship to creation, or the creator. As such, our individual consciousness is always changing as we discover more about ourselves and gain a deeper understanding of our role, purpose and relationship with and to the whole of creation. There is always one more step in our unfoldment to a greater awareness of this relationship. However, while this growth of consciousness is an individual matter, the changes made on an individual level eventually affect the whole, and our society has already reached a critical mass in spirituality and the adoption of Spiritual Values.

It is a fact that when a product or idea reaches one percent acceptance in a society, it moves to rapid adoption. There are numerous examples of how a shift in consciousness occurs when a critical mass is reached. We have seen examples of the phenomenon in the introduction of new products, political ideas, music styles, design and color trends. When approximately one percent adoption is reached, the concept, idea or product takes on mass adoption and a trend is undeniable.

We have reached that critical mass and a rapid adoption of Spiritual Values has begun. As such, our consciousness is shifting as a society, and we are taking a major step. I call this step the Millennium Shift. This shift in consciousness is happening as we adopt new Spiritual Values as the guiding principles of our lives. It offers each of us the opportunity to move to a greater vision of who we are, what we can be and what is possible. As we become more aware of our relationship to the universe around us, we likewise become more aware of our possibilities as human beings. After 10 years of research, American sociologist Paul Ray, Ph.D., estimates the size of this group of early adoptors at 44 million people in the United States.

The Third Transition of Man

In the history of man there have been other significant transitions. The first was man's shift from hunter/gatherer to an agrarian society. With that transition, man moved from a survival mode in which he had little time to do anything but survive, to a society that had time to build villages, towns and other structures, the likes of which we take for granted today. The economic and time gains of this shift also produced a surplus that could support a priestcraft, and allowed most people to participate in formal religion for the first time. This entire shift from a hunter/gatherer to an agrarian society, took place slowly, over a long period of time and was supported and inspired by an accompanying shift in consciousness or awareness.

A second major shift occurred as man moved into the industrial age. This shift was accompanied by a more dramatic shift in consciousness, as the Renaissance era began and music and art reached heights of beauty and perfection never before seen. This age settled in much more quickly, over the period of two hundred years, and, again, mankind gained time to develop his creativity, both as individuals and as a society.

11

Today, the third transition of man is taking place. This transition, which some have called the "Age of the Individual" or the Age of Aquarius, began with the advent of the communications age in the early 1980s and the rapid adoption of the personal computer. Unlike previous transitions, it is occurring over a much shorter period of time. I would estimate that it will take only 40 to 50 years. It will cause major upheavals as we alter our very way of being and interacting with one another, in order to fully make use of the shift and the new technology. To do so, we will need to mature as a society, develop new levels of self-respect and respect for others, and be willing to work in greater harmony with our fellow man. In short, we will need to incorporate Spiritual Values into our lives, values that include giving others freedom and slowing down, both of which are subjects explored in the coming chapters.

The incorporation of these Spiritual Values into our lives will change forever the way we that we are. Essentially, this third transition represents another significant shift in consciousness. It is about discovering and seeing ourselves as spiritual beings more openly. And once again, this shift will bring with it the gift of more personal time—time that will give us an opportunity to reflect inwardly and pursue answers to some of our deepest questions.

Discovering Our True Identity

That is what this millennium shift in consciousness is all about. It is our recognizing that we are an inner being as well as an outer being, that there is a part of us that is greater than our minds can grasp presently. It deals with our inner urges and intuition. It is that part of us that is at our very core. Some call it our center or our heart. Others, including myself, call it Soul. But whatever we call it, we are coming to recognize that this inner part of us *is* our true self. The shift is about becoming more aware of this reality, that each of us is a spiritual being, or Soul. We are spiritual beings having a human experience. And as Soul we are a part of the whole, or the entirety of creation. We are actually an integral part of creation and a part of the creator. This is not a fact that we simply come to believe. It is something that without reservation, we come to *know*.

We are Here to Learn about Divine Love

Millions of people (or should I say Souls) are coming to the realization that we are all connected. Again, this is not something they are being asked to believe. It is an inner truth that is coming into focus. They are coming to understand that, as Soul, they are eternal and free. Soul is here in the physical body on earth to learn, to grow in awareness of its relationship with the creator, and ultimately to learn the true nature of love. This ultimate goal is referred to as God Realization by many in Eastern belief systems. However, there is a major step which must be taken before the God Realized state of awareness or consciousness is gained. That interim step is the full realization of oneself as Soul— referred to as Self Realization by many belief systems. As the shift to Spiritual Values takes place, these terms, Self-realization and God-realization, are becoming mainstream in Western cultures. We are learning that we are spiritual beings, a part of creation, on our way to learning how to love all life.

SYNOPSIS

Today, what is happening is that we are adopting a new set of values and are shifting to a new level of awareness or consciousness. This is uplifting the ability of millions of people to sense and understand that there is a greater truth to their lives, that they have a spiritual purpose, which is to learn and to grow. Our new Spiritual Values are the driving force in the new millennium and will be the cause of significant personal, workplace, institutional and world changes.

TRENDS AND IMPLICATIONS

* The spiritual is becoming an everyday topic of exploration and conversation.
* There is a greater expression of interest in who we are and why we are here. We are, in fact, seeking a better understanding of our spiritual nature and our true identity as spiritual beings, or Soul.
* Spirituality is acknowledged as a relevant force in the workplace.
* The adoption of Spiritual Values is expressed in our growing interest in support of various ecological causes, wellness and personal development programs, as well as in the transitioning to simpler lives.

CHAPTER TWO

The Networking of the Economy

As we begin the new millennium, we are witnessing one of the greatest changes mankind has ever experienced. This change is subtle but all encompassing. It is a result of our increasing awareness of who we are at our innermost being, and it is changing the way we think and relate to one another. In a word, it is changing our values. Indeed, it is changing and will continue to change everything in our world as our awareness of a new code of behavior becomes clearer and clearer. This new code of behavior, which can be defined in terms of living our lives in harmony with certain Spiritual Principles, will be evident in the new values we continue to adopt in the coming years. Many call these new values, Spiritual Values, and, as we embrace the new Spiritual Values and begin to live by them, our world will dramatically change.

Technological Revolution Brings Greater Freedom and Responsibility

Running parallel to this adoption of new values is a technological revolution, which is occurring as computing, telecommunications and networking innovations converge to deliver new services and capabilities. The new technology is altering forever the way we interact with one another and the world at large, both in our leisure pursuits and in our personal business, as well as the workplace. What we are actually witnessing is a networking of our economy, which will result in a greater degree of freedom for those who are willing to accept its attendant increase in responsibility. There is actually a direct correlation here, or an equation, between responsibility accepted and freedom gained.

As unique beings we have self-determination, but many in the industrial age gave up this freedom, in varying degrees, to others, such as their employers, spouses, or the government, in exchange for the security provided by the relationship. They placed responsibility for their lives in someone else's hands. This phenomenon of placing responsibility for one's life in someone else's hands is at the root of the government-owes-me-a-living syndrome which has been so prevalent in recent history. Part of the spiritual evolution now taking place, however, is a strong move toward regaining our identity as Soul. The outcome is expressed as sovereignty. We want to be in control of our lives and our destinies, and we are willing to take responsibility for the freedom this gives us, without having to lean unduly on other individuals or institutions to run our lives. The e-commuting movement, enabled by the networked economy, is actually being fueled by this new sense of responsibility and a desire for greater freedom, which, together, constitute sovereignty.

Freedom and Control through E-Commuting

The flexibility that thousands of individuals are achieving in their work time and place is a growing trend. More and more today, people are taking advantage of the opportunity to work from home or a non-traditional workplace. This trend will continue to grow with the addition of video to the Internet, when bandwidth and cost reductions converge shortly to deliver economical video communications solutions.

The whole shift to home offices and e-commuting for employees is actually being created by our spiritual advancement, and the movement is an expression of our need to be our own caretaker. The networked worker can set his own timetable and work at any hour of the day or night. The freedom so gained is a direct reflection of the responsibility accepted. In the not so distant future, the urge for this newfound flexibility and freedom will become a dominant factor in our economy, as the "eco generation" (the children of the boomers) begin to drive the new economy in the next seven years. Having grown up with both technology and an incredible new level of freedom of communication, created by remarkable access to a broad range of media and the Internet, this group will drive technological solutions we cannot envision from our current vantage point today.

The Economy is Delayering

In the decades to come, the entire economy and our basic social movements and behavior will be driven by the desire for freedom. We will work from home or satellite sites much of the time, sell our services via video conference, and interact with our personal service suppliers such as the neighborhood grocery store or fast food outlet, via electronic means. Our productivity will also increase as we move into an economy that contains less friction and fewer layers.

In the 1990s, free trade agreements began to prepare the world for a new freedom of movement. The result, in this new decade, as this freedom expands, will be a more efficient or ecological world as we trade globally, and the distance between buyer and seller will shorten or disappear altogether, as e-services offer direct access to what we need in a timely and cost-efficient manner. As a result, we will not be paying for unnecessary middlemen in transactions, nor will we require fancy packaging as an incentive to get us to pick certain products off the shelf. Instead, with the continued growth of electronic shopping, the packaging will be electronically produced to capture our attention while we browse or shop on-line. The world as a whole will benefit from this shift, as less of the earth's resources are used to create packaging, and we will be able to reduce and reuse more efficiently.

The trickledown effects of this shift will effect the production of many goods over the next twenty years, as we reduce overall demand in the economy for these items. Already, the use of auction sites is offering bargains to Internet users and this can easily extend to personal or corporately used goods, with nothing being wasted. The overall result of delayering will be a greater degree of efficiency and economy in all of our personal and business interactions.

The Just-In-Time Personal World

This increased efficiency and economy will also affect our personal lives in significant ways, with future technology making it easier for us to order our lives around the just-in-time philosophy which is now taking hold in the manufacturing sector. We will be able to easily acquire what we need, when we need it, and with little effort. The need to retain items will therefore lose favor in a new less-is-better world. So, whereas the old paradigm has been to hold on to possessions for up to a lifetime (a very inefficient use of the earth's resources), the new world will allow us to only possess what we need at any particular point in time.

Spiritually, the shift is toward economy and ecology, and toward ordering our lives around the principle of voluntary simplicity, for our own health and that of the planet.

Teamwork Goes Hand-in-Hand with Specialization

We will also be able to work with greater efficiency within the work world. To do so, however, requires a change in how we work, since, as the pace of change gets faster and faster, it will be impossible to know everything or have all of the information on any given topic. In fact, many people are burning out right now just from trying to keep up.

To offset the natural inclination to keep up with the pace, there is an emerging trend toward slowing down. This decelerating automatically invokes the need for teamwork. We will have to become specialists and share our expertise in teams. Ironically, this slower pace is actually more productive by virtue of the greater access to creativity that is gained. Slowing down allows us to come up with better solutions to our problems and difficulties and to make the right choices as to which tasks we address in our day. The biggest gain, however, is a reduction in stress, better work attendance and, for the individual, a more relaxed and a more contented life.

A New Family Dynamic of Teamwork

The team approach also applies to the family unit. The role of all family members will change as spouses and children develop their own areas of expertise. For example, in my house, my son is already the technology expert. My partner is the health and fitness expert, and I have the entertainment and travel focus. Everyone makes a valuable contribution. This shift toward a team dynamic will have a dramatic effect on the new family and the spiritual value of respect will extend to all, regardless of age or gender, socially as well as in the workplace.

Our children will be, and already are, interacting with the world in a way we could not have imagined even a few years ago. They are, for example, operating services on the Internet and entertaining themselves with global friends via networked games. One World is reality for our children. They are used to it and expect it. They will also be able to access (and many are) any information they want, including censored material. This includes information of a sexual or violent nature, as well as information which we consider to be dangerous (e.g., information on making bombs). Nonetheless, everything is now available for all to see. Censorship is dead in the new networked world, but it is being replaced with a new spiritual value set, which includes freedom gained through responsibility, the use of individual discretion, and the ability to decide for ourselves what constitutes right action or behavior.

In response, we will advance toward a new way of counseling our children, as we move into the new millennium. Rather than simply saying "no", we will offer a valid rationale to help our children make decisions on their own. As parents, the best thing we will do for our children in the uncensored world is to acknowledge the world as it is, with all of its positive and negative elements. We can then teach our children the truth about what is of value in this world and guide them in forming their own personal value set.

Truth and Nothing But the Truth

The new openness created by an electronic playing field, to which all have access, will also effect the realm of public service and government and usher in a new era in which only the truth will do—truth in both political motives and in action. There will be a higher degree of accountability as the actions and misactions of both corporations and the government will be visible for all to see. Media spin and government cover-ups will become increasingly difficult to pull off as we shift to a more open world of communication. The bottom line is that honesty will be a requirement and a natural outcome of the shift to Spiritual Values.

SYNOPSIS

As the networked economy takes hold, our spiritual evolution will create significant shifts in the way that we work and interact with the world at large. We will gain freedom as we have never had before and will be able to work at any time and with only those whom we choose. It does not matter whether we are old or young, deaf or blind, living in wealth or frugally, or located in Montana or Sweden. When on the Internet, we will be judged only by our interaction electronically. We will meet friends we could never see in person and we will be able to recreate at any time of the day with complete freedom.

E-commerce is also enabling us to interact and transact from wherever we are, with anyone, anywhere on the globe. As we move deeper into the new economy, we will gain freedom in equal measure to the responsibility we accept for our lives. Our productivity will increase as the layers of interaction are removed and there is less friction in the economy and in the way we interact to buy and sell products and services. We will require and desire fewer possessions and need to store less information in our heads as just-in-time delivery of information, goods and services become a further reality. We will also find ourselves moving automatically toward a team dynamic, which will allow us to work with greater efficiency and to manage the increased pace and flow of information, both at work and at home.

All these changes are being fueled not only by the current technological revolution, but by our increasing shift to a Spiritual Values driven economy. In fact, the very values of the Internet itself are an expression of the spiritual freedom we are seeking. It is an open, self-policed world where all may express their views. It provides tremendous freedom, but that freedom comes with its attendant responsibilities. Thus, as we move further into this new era, each individual—including government officials—will increasingly be required to interact with others in accordance to a new code of behavior, one built on Spiritual Values such as truth, fairness, openness and honesty.

TRENDS AND IMPLICATIONS

The Trend to E-Commuting
* The shift to home offices and decentralized work places will continue to provide the freedom to set our own timetables and place of work. This shift is being fueled by technology combined with a desire for freedom and responsibility.
* The trend movement is toward gaining control over our lives versus placing responsibility in the hands of government or others.
* There will be a universal respect extended to all on the Internet, regardless of whether they are old or young, rich or poor, physically challenged, male or female.

E-commerce

* Video interaction will propel the development of e-commerce.
* The delayering of the economy will create greater efficiency and productivity. Unnecessary middlemen will no longer be a part of the process.
* Freer trade will follow the 90s developments.
* New personal freedom of movement will follow.

Product Production

* We will use less packaging as we move to electronic product presentation via e-commerce.
* Recycling of products personally and corporately will increase, facilitated by auctions and on-line markets.

Trend to Simplicity

* We will move to just-in-time information, products and services.
* As used goods gain in value, we will recycle more. Buying clubs and recycling services will aid in the acquisition and divestiture process. New lending clubs will reduce the need to own.

Personal Specialization

* Information overload is moving us to become experts in our chosen areas.
* This leads to teamwork in the workplace and at home.

Openness and Truth

* Corporate and government action will be visible for all to see. Honesty will be required.
* Media spin and government concealments will be more difficult as we shift to an open world of communication.

CHAPTER THREE

The Sovereign Individual

The sovereign, or self-sufficient individual, is one more outcome of the new spiritual force, expressed as Spiritual Values, entering the world. The sovereign individual will be operating on these new values in order to be in harmony with, and thrive within, the networked economy. In fact, the shift in the new economy is actually a reflection of our inner need as Spiritual beings to be responsible for our own destiny. The effects of our move to individual sovereignty will be seen in the way we conduct ourselves, the way we socialize and interact with others, the products we buy and the way we buy them, as well as how we work and play. Ultimately, it will affect our expectations of government, as we move to being more responsible and self-sustaining.

Many elements in our shift to being sovereign individuals will evolve over the next ten years and radically alter our world. At the heart of this change, however, is a search for greater freedom and control and an increasing understanding of our true inner nature, which leads to a greater sense of responsibility in our lives. We are learning that we can create our lives and that we are no longer restricted by the expectations of others, by our upbringing, or any other factor for that matter.

We are Beginning to Create Our Lives

The networked economy will allow us to take even more control of our lives and will give us a tremendous degree of flexibility over the location and time of our activities. This will allow us to work and play according to our own natural rhythms and flow of life. No longer will we need to fit into the 9-to-5 mold. Instead, we will increasingly be able to work on our own time schedules and to assume greater responsibility for our work efforts and lives, as a whole.

Interestingly, as we begin to accept greater responsibility for ourselves and for the creation of our lives, the rise of the sovereign individual will correspond with the demise of the victim mentality. More and more we will begin to understand the futility of blaming others for our lives. We are not victims of circumstances. Though this may be hard for some people to accept, we are totally responsible for the condition of our own lives and, at some level, we are actually growing in just the right way from all of our circumstances, even the trials and difficulties we all face. There is tremendous power to be regained in our lives from this realization, which will allow us to fulfill our dreams to a much greater degree. We will then be able to truly create our lives and to do so with less government intervention, because, in the end, governments will serve the people on the people's terms.

Sovereignty Shifts from Government to the Individual

Indeed, as the networked economy takes hold, we will see a shift to wanting less government. This will occur not because government will want to give up power, but because we will be seeking to take greater responsibility for ourselves. We will therefore decrease our reliance on others, including governments, for all that we need. Privatization is one of the first visible signs of this trend.

Sovereignty will also shift from nations to the individual as the networked world increasingly conducts its affairs globally and governments lose control of their tax bases as they are now structured. The number of people joining the ranks of the globally employed will grow exponentially in the next ten years, creating a groundswell of change that will enhance our individual sovereignty. Such people, working in virtual environments, will earn income globally, bank their money globally, and compete in a global economy, without the same need for governments to serve or protect them with legislation.

Governments, for their part, will find it increasingly difficult to collect taxes on income in a global economy where income can be earned and banked in other jurisdictions. This change is in line with the new Spiritual Values, which offers individuals greater personal choice in managing their lives. Eventually, in response to these changes, taxation will be focused on consumption versus income. The rewards will go to the entrepreneurial-minded individual and to the worker.

The spiritual shift behind this change is the recognition that we are, at our core, a part of creation and that there is a part of us, an inner part that some call Soul, that is here to learn and become more aware. As we learn more about our true selves, we begin to know that we have to stand on our own two feet and take responsibility for our lives.

Self Responsibility Leads to a Decline in Free Rides

One natural result of the coming changes in this direction will be the decline of the free ride for able-bodied individuals who are currently living off society. The sovereign individual,

27

living according to Spiritual Values, accepts full responsibility for his life and his welfare. The emphasis in social welfare will therefore shift slowly to helping all members of society take responsibility for their lives. Education and moving assistance will be favored in order to help those who require assistance to restore their lives to productivity. Such assistance will be given, however, only for the time they are in transition.

Eventually, all members of society will make a positive contribution in their own way and within their capabilities. E-commerce will help make this possible, from training and re-education, to enabling those who are unable to leave their homes or regions to provide services from the home.

Work and Play Begin to Merge

On a somewhat lighter note, the shift to individual sovereignty will also manifest as an increasing desire for personal expression. One visible, though seemingly innocuous sign of this shift is the movement to casual dress in the workplace. The rigid dress code of the industrial age—suits, ties and conservative attire—is giving way to a more flexible expression of our individuality and we are now being allowed to create our own look to a much greater extent than the workaday world has hitherto allowed.

The casual dress code, which was once allowable only in a few professions, like advertising agencies, has taken hold in high tech (creative) environments and will likely be adopted in the workplace as a whole in the next few years. This shift to casual dress will be a sure way to distinguish advanced working environments that foster creative expression by blending work and play together. The ideal end point will be for all of us to feel a sense of satisfaction from our work to such a degree that the definition of work actually changes. For many, it will no longer be work per se, but will be seen as the time we spend in our income-producing role, as the flow of life allows us to create with effortless effort.

Fashion Becomes Lifestyle

As the demand for individual expression expands and technology allows for customization at lower costs, we will continue to see more expressions of individuality both in the workplace and at large. As we begin the new millennium, youth fashion is, as usual, in non-conformance with the previous generation, but we are now seeing signs of even greater degrees of personal expression than displayed by previous generations. What we are witnessing, on the whole, is a major trend toward personalization, including one-of-a-kind objects and clothing.

This individualization of fashion and its expression of lifestyle will lead to the phenomenon of tribal cultures based on fashion. By this I mean that the trend of cultural conformity will continue to give way to a proud display of the various cultural heritages which make up our society. Already, a growing number of people have begun to celebrate their cultural heritage in the clothing they wear, their hairstyles and, in some cases, in a return to an indigenous language. This new sense of confidence will continue to replace the previously felt need to conform and blend in. In short, people will not be afraid to be who they are.

This growing phenomenon is a reflection of the search for an outer identity that is an expression of our inner uniqueness as a spiritual being. Technologically, it is being supported by the trend of mass customization, which allows products to be produced to our exact specifications, in order to meet our need to express our personal identity.

Taking Control of Our Lives and Our Health

The increased desire to express our individuality, combined with a greater sense of personal responsibility, is also the driving force behind our mass shift to health and fitness. Today, we are healthier and fitter than we have ever been. This is especially true for those over 50. By and large, we are eating better and taking better care of ourselves than any other time in recent history. There are dramatic changes taking place with the reduction of smoking and the limitations being placed on where smoking is permitted. Changes in the consumption of alcohol are also underway, with lighter drinks and non-alcoholic versions of traditional cocktails gaining popularity.

Another sign of this swing to greater self-responsibility for our own well being can be found in the increasing use of self-diagnostic tests and the growing participation in wellness programs, which has moved from the personal market to the workplace. Following this same trend line, we will likely see an increase in the travel options being offered for wellness/spa vacations and spiritual retreats. The health food industry will also continue its rapid growth as we search for pure products and foods with fewer additives, better nutrient content, and unique health attributes.

Individualized Lifestyles Go to the Edge

There is also a growing interest in personal and participatory sports, which we can enjoy on our own timetable. Witness the recent explosion in unique activities in which one can now participate, such as in-line skating, skate and snow boarding, rock climbing, and white water rafting, a sport for all ages. In fact, the sport of mountain biking has not only come into its own in the last ten years, it has now been divided into three distinct sports: extreme, trail thrashing, and recreational.

In the same time frame, the new industry of personal training has risen, complete with certification programs and national associations. One American fitness club has a policy of providing each of its members with a personal trainer. However, if a member expresses any negative comments about their previous personal trainer or asks for a guarantee, they are denied club membership. This club knows that this type of person is not taking responsibility for their life and is seeking to blame others for their progress or lack of it. Such a person cannot be helped in this new club environment which was created specifically for the self-motivated individual who takes responsibility for his or her own life.

All these sports and activities are expressions of our search for our true identity, and this trend will grow in the new decade. But the trend is not limited to the arena of sports. Entertainment choices are also expanding to reflect our many individual tastes. Multi-screen cinemas, the multiplicity of television channels, and the variety of periodicals is a testament to our need to be served by life on our terms. The old mediums are giving way to specialty information and entertainment providers that we select based on our specific needs and interests.

The arts are likewise experiencing a renaissance as demand increases for personal expression and we slow down enough to want to appreciate the real things in life. Flower sales are up and will continue to rise as our appreciation of nature grows. We are becoming global travelers, exploring more distant lands and we are looking for adventure customized to our personal interests, which may range from other cultures to archeology and from scenic beauty and wildlife to religious tours. As we pursue these interests, we will find ourselves living our lives with a greater sense of passion and excitement than ever before.

Living Our Own Lives

In the industrial age it was not uncommon to live life through the experiences of another, such as a spouse or a child. One person would put their own life and needs on hold and give all of their attention to another. As a result, the person led a life that was off balance and unfulfilled. However, as we move into the new Spiritual Values age, this concept of living a life through another will be increasingly abandoned in favor of full lives, in which we first fulfill our own needs and then reach out to give to others.

We will discover in ever increasing numbers that the key to truly loving another is that we must first love ourselves. This means taking care of our own needs because we cannot truly help others to grow spiritually and lead contented, fulfilling lives unless we ourselves first set the example. This realization will make for a more balanced approach to living and lead to a much improved and more fulfilling lifetime experience. Then, even when it feels like we are trying to push water up hill, we will search for ways that move us back into the flow of life and reconnect us with ourselves.

Self Respect Leads to Greater Respect for Others

Ultimately, our greater sense of individuality, self-responsibility and self-respect will have positive results on those around us as well, both in our work environment and in our personal relationships. The Spiritual Values of trust, openness, respect, listening, honesty, forgiveness and caring will take on new meaning and will enrich our relationship experiences as we allow ourselves to redefine our lives in the next ten years.

We will begin to move with the new flow and a new level

of respect for others will take hold. We will not necessarily like everyone we encounter but we will at least have an impersonal good will for everyone. In other words, we will respect each person for the journey they are on and the lessons they are learning. After all, everyone is unique. We are the sum total of our past experiences, and these past experiences are shaping our lessons today in this schoolhouse called Earth. So, what might be easy for us to do may be supremely difficult for another, and vice versa. Understanding this allows us to cultivate greater degrees of compassion and acceptance for others.

In the work realm, this will translate as a greater respect for our co-workers or employees, their contributions and ideas. It will also be seen in a genuine desire and respect for the female perspective by businesses, which will be looking for better alternatives in the way they structure and deliver products and services to the market.

The Evolution of Relationships

This trend will similarly transform our personal relationships. Significantly, as part of the shift to a Spiritual Values driven society, we will see a major trend towards forming real friendships before we have intimate relations. Such friends can always talk to each other, they respect each other and are true partners, which provides a strong basis for a lasting relationship.

The beginnings of this trend can already be seen in our youth, who have a much better rapport with members of the opposite sex. Girls call the boys as well as the other way around. They are friends and hang out with each other to a much greater extent than the preceding generation. This generation will form long-term relationships on the basis of being friends first. This trend will spread to the older generations as well, with more relationships in the new millennium being formed on a foundation of communication, with each partner having a genuine interest in the welfare of the other. In such relationships, we will serve our partners by listening and by better communicating our feelings, rather than burying them only to have them possibly resurface in built-up anger at a later time. We will also develop greater trust in our relationships, through communication, which will lead to freedom of action.

Loving is Giving Freedom and Letting Go

For many, the concept of partners for life is also changing with the shift to the adoption of Spiritual Values. Individuals will have the potential to grow spiritually in the new millennium at a faster rate than in the old industrial age consciousness. However, the fact is that we may not always grow together or at the same rate as our partner. We will therefore find ourselves in relationships for as long as they are helping us grow, but when they no longer serve our inner need for growth, our inner nudges and intuition will move us on to develop either on our own or with another partner.

It was two years after my own divorce that I grasped the truth of this principle myself and came to understand that both my wife and I had needed the change in order to allow us to grow and blossom in our own individual ways. This growth was neither possible nor likely for either of us within the construct of the marriage, with all of the built up expectations we had both created in the relationship.

We can learn a lot about love from understanding this principle. We are actually loving someone by giving them the opportunity to be, to act, and to create in their own way without interference or undue influence. We love by giving space to others. We let them grow in their own way and learn from their mistakes. In the movie industry, the process of filmmaking is a series of " miss takes" and so it is with our lives. And so the ultimate form of love is non-interference.

Eventually, we will learn to let go of those we love, when either we or they need to move into greater opportunities for growth. This is a part of true service and love for another. It means giving them their freedom to express their life in their own way. In time, society will come to acknowledge this process as being as natural as the changes in the seasons and amicable partings will come to replace the industrial age "divorce from hell" scenario so many have suffered.

This is by no means, however, to suggest that lifelong commitments are impossible or should not be a worthy goal. In fact, as individuals come to know themselves and their own spiritual journey better, it is more likely that they will choose partners who are truly compatible with them and who share their larger vision. A union of this nature will be the joining of two whole sovereign individuals, rather than two incomplete halves, each seeking completion through the other. In such marriages, the focus will then be on what each person can offer the other, and on what the couple, together, can offer the world.

SYNOPSIS

The new Spiritual Values are changing our view of who we are and how we associate with others. As we embrace our true spiritual nature, we naturally assume responsibility for our thoughts, words and deeds and their effect on others. We learn that we are responsible for our lives and not the government or some other person or institution. And, as we grow in our responsibility, we will be given freedom in equal measure to the responsibility we assume—freedom to work, play, and relax when we desire. These changes mark the emergence of the sovereign individual, who is empowered, self-sustaining and in control of his or her own life.

It is this shift to individual sovereignty and greater personal responsibility that is reflected in our increased desire for personal expression. What we are searching for is an outer identity that is as unique to us as our inner, spiritual identity. We want the ability to create our own lives and express our individuality in our own way. No longer are we part of the herd. We are increasingly making our own choices and will continue to express our individuality in more obvious ways in the new millennium. What this means is that we will be leading and creating full, exciting lives for ourselves, which reflect our individual interests and desires.

Naturally, these changes will have an affect on our relationships as well, and, as we begin to realize that we are here to learn and grow, we will also focus on Spiritual Values in our interaction with others. At work this will manifest as a greater respect for those we work with and in our personal relationships, we are moving toward a foundation of respect and communication which allows us to truly honor our partner. This translates into a friends-first approach to beginning relationships, but also entails a change in our expectation of relationships and our willingness to grant freedom to our partners.

All of these changes are a reflection of our individual sovereignty as we move toward individual alignment with the Spiritual Values, freedom and responsibility, that are facilitated by the networked economy.

TRENDS AND IMPLICATIONS

Sovereignty Shifts to the Individual

* The networked economy will give us greater flexibility (location, time, activities) in our work. This freedom is a reflection of our spiritual need to be responsible for ourselves and our lives.

* More individuals are joining and will continue to join the ranks of the globally employed, who earn and bank their funds globally.

* As a result of the shift to a global economy, taxes will eventually be focused on consumption rather than on income, resulting in greater rewards for the entrepreneur and the worker.

Self-Responsibility

* As we assume more personal responsibility, we will be seeking less government and fewer services.

* Welfare programs will shift to providing transitional help for given time frames, in order to help all individuals to make a contribution.

* We are beginning to make our own choices independent of mass thought. As sovereign individuals we will create greater flexibility for ourselves. Our old rigid codes and concepts will give way to the ability to create our lives.

Lifestyle Shifts

* For many, there will be a redefinition of work, as work and play are integrated and we move to an effortless form of work.

* Casual dress codes will gain increasing acceptance, an indication of less rigidity, which will lead to changes in the definition of work.

* A new respect for the uniqueness in everyone will lead to advances in personal expression, with fashion statements being made by our clothing, hairstyles, etc.

* We will continue to express our individuality and gain greater control over our personal environment in the next decade. This personal expression is our search for an outer identity that is as unique to us as our inner Spiritual identity.

* Personalization is being reflected in one-of-a-kinds and, in the next decade, will be enabled by mass customization. We will see greater personalization and individualization of our lives in our activities, sports, and associations. There will be an expansion of new sports, the arts and wellness. The interest in personal sports will continue, with the extreme-challenge sports edge expanding rapidly.

* Entertainment is fragmenting and expanding to reflect individual tastes. The Internet will enable the entertainment market of one with just-in-time downloads and viewing of music and video. We will witness a continuing explosion of periodicals, multi-screen cinema, satellite TV and new music styles. Specialty information provided via Internet will be delivered, customized to specific tastes, and delivered when we want it. Already one can customize a CD with only the

songs desired. In the next 10 years, we will be able to download music a la carte.

Relationship Trends

* We will look for a deeper kind of relationship. More relationships will start as friendship.

* The new relationship foundation will be communication versus sex. We will become better communicators as we get in touch with our feelings and communicate them freely. We will then solve relationship problems with dialogue and begin to serve our partners by listening.

* We will pursue our individual interests within relationships and will give each other space to develop separate hobbies, sports, social agenda, and vacations.

* Relationships will work because both partners will be growing in the relationship. If growth ceases, we will recognize that it is time to change. The greater recognition of our own needs in the new decade will allow us to see when we have outgrown a relationship. Relationship changes will be a lot easier in the new millennium. We will let each other go out of love and amicable partings will be a major trend.

CHAPTER FOUR

The Metamorphosis of Retailing

There are several trends that point to a radically different world of retailing in the new millennium. These trends, which are driven by our new Spiritual Values and the new enabling technology, constitute a direct response to our increased desire to express our individuality and uniqueness as sovereign individuals. As these factors combine to transform the retailing world, the changes will be nowhere more evident than in the emerging e-retail (or "e-tail") environment.

The Internet Becomes as Accessible as the Telephone

One obvious factor that will contribute to the e-tail boom to come is the incredible increase in Internet participation. Access to the Internet is undergoing a rapid expansion, as millions of users are connecting to free advertising supported services. There are also new access technologies, such as telephone and TV set applications, which will further reduce the cost of access and expand participation. Pair this with the rapidly falling cost of computers, as millions gain access to the technology, and access becoming even more attainable. In fact, the new inexpensive hand held or palm computers are now all a person needs to access the Internet. The critical mass of users is therefore a key velocity component of the millennium shift.

Customization to the Individual

As more and more people gain access to the Internet and use it more frequently, the new World Wide Web portals will attract consumers with their richness of services, entertainment value, customizable information, and relevance to our needs. Consumers will also be able to set their computer screens to show only the services and product categories that are of interest to them, and retailers will strive to make their portals as sticky as possible with unique services and functionality.

Most major portals are now able to track user areas of interest via all of the sites users visit. They can then produce a dynamic environment of specific relevance to the consumer, through customization of advertising and content. As consumers, we will consequently only see advertising on the portal for products in which we have shown an interest (as tracked by our travels on the web). The information sections will also highlight content that is derived from the sites visited or that is based on user specified requests.

For some, privacy of information will be a concern with this new system. However, the new tracking systems on the Internet do not attach the web visit and purchase information to a user's personal data, such as name, address or telephone number. The data is only used in aggregated form, thereby eliminating privacy intrusions. Ultimately, I believe that the average consumer will feel that the benefits provided by this dynamic marketing system, which delivers greater relevance to their needs in a timely fashion, will outweigh the possible risk of the information being used for unethical purposes.

Advertising Becomes Relevant

The advertising model that supports the free Internet services is an extension of this customized marketing strategy. It is actually the pinnacle of the concept of marketing to the market of one, the individual, as advertising becomes directed only at those who have demonstrated an interest in the subject, product or service. This is possible because, as touched on above, the portal will be able to track all destinations visited on the Internet and all purchases made, as well as the length of browsing time, time of day, and virtually any other data that is useful. The result is a system that responds to the consumer's individual needs.

This one-to-one marketing is very economical and efficient for the advertiser, and quite valuable and non-intrusive for the consumer. The consumer only sees relevant services or product offers and advertising in which they have a demonstrated interest. The information is even timed to when they need it. In fact, the new shopping environment will actually anticipate the needs of the consumer. This concept of delivering just-in-time information, products and services is moving shopping from a push to a pull strategy, by allowing consumers to pull from the system what they need, when they need it, rather than having information constantly pushed at them, regardless of its relevance. Consequently, as we progress into the electronic shopping era, we will no longer need to put the same effort into shopping, and the marketing of products and services will no longer be based on inefficient mass marketing. Instead, it will be highly focused on the needs of the consumer, who will gain a new freedom of being able to shop anytime, anywhere.

Buying, Selling and Borrowing Made Easy

In the new millennium, new services will also help us to buy and divest ourselves of unwanted things. These services save us time and allow us to make better choices, as opposed to ill-informed decisions. There is an important distinction to be made between choices and decisions. Decisions are made with limited information, but, the more information we have, the more our decision becomes a choice. This is particularly significant since the mass consumerism and spending for the sheer pleasure of shopping, which hit a peak in the late 80s, is dying fast. It is being replaced with a careful attention to quality, service and overall value. Over the next ten years or so, with access to e-retail consumer options, buying will be elevated to a fine art and we can look for product differentiators to expand into the areas of service follow-up, with guarantees around quality, longevity, recyclability, and easy return policies in case of dissatisfaction. The new buying services will allow us to compare value, price and all of these factors, thereby enabling us to make better choices as consumers.

The development of on-line auctions, in particular, will create a major shopping mode for significant purchases at great prices. As this shopping format expands to encompass a broad range of services and products, pricing will become razor sharp due to global competition among retailers and the auction services. The use of these auctions and service programs will also make it easier for us to divest ourselves of unwanted items. We will be able to consign our goods to electronic auction houses and see our items sold on worldwide virtual markets for any specific item. This will likewise make it easier to purchase used items and will create a great market in used items. As a result, prices of quality used items will rise. With this in mind, we will evaluate our purchases on the basis of residual as well as initial value.

This trend will also enable us to easily let go of and acquire whatever we need. This approach is both economical and ecological and, as we move more deeply into the new economy, we will never need to own more than what we need at any particular time, nor will we hang on to unwanted items. We will lead less-cluttered lives and, as we recycle more, there will be a great shift in the production of goods, with reconditioning services growing to fill the need and demand for quality used goods.

In keeping with this ecological trend, we will also own less and share more. Community services will spring up around the concept of sharing, and club or community groups will create pools of items, like garden tools or seasonal items, which are better borrowed than owned. As a result of this new form of sharing, a sense of community that some religious or spiritual communities have such as the Mennonites and the Amish will be rekindled. This, in turn, will further reduce demand for new manufactured goods.

Delayering Means Fewer Middlemen

When we do buy, the new e-commerce systems and buying services will allow us to shop direct, removing several layers of distribution and transshipment from the process. As we move into the electronic shopping mode, we will transition to buying from the manufacturer for many major items, since brokers and dealers will not be able to add significant enough value in the exchange process to warrant the extra cost of their involvement. Some refer to this delayering of the economy as a frictionless economy, in which there is no distance between the buyer and the seller/

manufacturer. A graphic example of this transition can be seen in the company, Dell Computers, which now sells direct to the buyer over the Internet and by telephone, cutting out jobbers and retailers from the distribution chain. The travel industry is making a similar transition to direct sales and there is no longer the same need for brokers of many such services, including certain kinds of insurance.

The role of the retailer will also change dramatically, in this process, and many retailers will only survive as portals, or places where consumers enter the Internet. They will provide the services relevant to the needs of the consumer through the design of electronic environments that are customized to the consumer's specified needs. Large retailers will be front-end electronic merchandisers (places you visit for convenience and entertainment on the Internet) and they will be back-end distribution centers, providing services to consumers and other retailers as well. These large retailers will also coordinate delivery through specialty delivery organizations, and many will share ownerships in these organizations as part of a vertically-integrated retail system on a global scale.

Global Retailing

The first signs of global retailing are emerging with the launch of GloboGift, a worldwide gift service <www.globogift.com> comprised of represented retailers in major countries. The next step is a global alliance of retailers similar to the airline alliances that are now in place. In the future, an American consumer will be able to shop on an Italian web site for Venetian glass ornaments, and the Italian retailer will send the purchase order to an American alliance retailer partner for local fulfillment.

Competition for the customer dollar will be global, as well, and will first be evident on the Internet in the arena of services which are digitized, such as financial services, music and videos. These services can now be delivered (downloaded) quickly via the Internet due to drops in the cost of computing power and bandwidth expansion. Such digital-based services will lead the way, followed by consulting services and other services which can be easily ordered electronically, for example travel and entertainment categories and the related ticketing. With this change, the bricks and mortar travel agency of the future will focus on specialty requirements and will deliver personal service either over the telephone or in person.

The Micro Financial Transaction Arrives

The shopping paradigm of the new millennium will also be propelled forward by microchip card technology, which will enable the introduction of micro purchases. Consumers can now load cash onto a micro chip in a card and pay for goods, telephone calls and other services in many areas of the world today. Use of such cards is rapidly expanding in many campus settings.

American Express was first to introduce their chip-enabled card to facilitate Internet commerce transactions. Computers are now being produced with a chip-card port. A host of new services will spring up, as previously mentioned, to provide the consumer with vital product and service information such as product ratings and value comparisons. These services will be sold for small amounts—tenths of a cent in some cases and up to a dollar or more in others—and the chip card will facilitate the payment in a secure fashion. This new technology will allow us to make better use of our time as we shop for information, services and products in the electronic world.

We can also expect to see authentication or validation services spring up, in order to protect us from fraudulent offers, false web sites and shoddy services and products, which will no doubt also be present. Such seal of approval and authentication services will stand to make major gains, by providing this new and necessary service.

The Retailer Transforms

As a result of these many changes, the retailer that we know today will be radically altered over the next ten years. Our physical world shopping expeditions will become more entertainment oriented as we shift our commodities shopping to on-line. The convenience of on-line shopping for everyday essentials will be exceptional, with the additional benefit of shopping basket price comparison services and our own personalized tracking system which will predict our consumption of every household item and electronically prompt us to reorder. Depending on a customer's chosen lifestyle, the need to actually visit a store may be reduced to the need only to pick up an order.

As an example of these trends, Hudson's Bay Company, Canada' largest department store chain, has announced plans to divide its Bay chain into two kinds of bricks and mortar services. The first they call the "Experience" store, a destination where you can purchase the broadest range of brands typical to downtown city locations. These stores will become more "entertainment" oriented in order to create a continued desirability of the in-person shopping experience. The other stores will offer the suburban shopper a quicker shopping trip, with streamlined product lines in a quality department store setting. The Experience format will continue to serve consumers needs for personal shopping, while the Express format will lend itself to supporting e-retail purchasing and local pick-up of goods, where home delivery is not available or desired.

I believe the future will continue to support the Experience format that Hudson's Bay is developing, but that the suburban model will decline as a retail format, as electronic shopping expands. Mass merchandisers have the most to loose and the greatest need to change. Leaders like Wal-Mart are launching Internet based shopping with complete backend pick and pack order fulfillment and delivery.

The Experience format will also be employed in malls, in a different way. Malls will likely transform into full community service centers in order to maintain their destination drawing power. The mall of the not-too-distant future will offer a one-stop experience akin to the old small town center. Redefined as entertainment centers, the major malls will offer a rich mix of dining, theater, thrill rides, video games, bowling, libraries, and a host of meeting places for all ages. They will also serve as pick-up depots for goods ordered on the Internet.

Customer Loyalty Becomes Relationship Management

With all of these changes, consumer loyalty will become particularly important to retailers, and will constitute a new marketing focus as the customer relationship takes on a multidimensional context. Retailers will want to maintain customer relationships over the lifetime of the customer and will track customer behavior throughout the life cycle to maintain and manage an ongoing dialogue with the customer. As a result of this change, the old loyalty points programs of the 1990s will be subordinated to programs that take a wholistic view of the customer and the total consumer relationship.

Marketers will likewise look at the complete customer

49

relationship, including such factors as the relevance of offers presented to the customer, the timing, non-intrusiveness, ease of shopping and fulfillment time, as well as quality of goods, guarantees and ease of product return. At the same time, the move to a communications based economy is ushering in a new era of truth in advertising and product manufacturing. The promotion of the 1980s, characterized by the hype of sweepstakes, games and scratch and wins, has been in decline throughout the 1990s. This hype is fading in favor of honesty and those who make unsubstantiated claims are seeing the swiftness of public reaction. As an example, Volvo's advertising, showing a car that did not crush under the weight of another vehicle, was deemed by the public to be misleading and was soon withdrawn.

The public is looking for genuine value, not smoke and mirrors. The new trend is moving in favor of value-added promotions. This trend will continue in the coming years as promotions give way to customer relationship programs that not only reward immediate purchase with a genuine value, but also reward the continuing loyalty of the customer over the longer timeframe, creating a life-long bond.

The calculation of the lifetime value of a customer will enable retailers to take a long-range view of the relationship and adjust their value proposition to reflect the overall value of the relationship. The retailer will know its customers at every stage of their lives and will structure its communications to maximize relevancy of offers to the customer's anticipated and demonstrated needs, via current purchasing patterns. The enormously wasteful mass communications methods such, as flyers, will rapidly decline as this one-to-one relationship marketing and permission marketing (newsletters, e-flyers etc., to which people choose to subscribe) proves to be more customer-friendly and cost-effective.

SYNOPSIS

The new Spiritual Values we are adopting are working in tandem with the technological changes to transform the retailing process and lead us to a new, more efficient world of relevant advertising. With the advent of the market of one, advertising of the future will be perceived more as information because of its relevance to our needs. Our new values, combined with the force of global competition, will also support an honest approach to pricing and product quality. This is particularly so since content and value will be exposed by vigilant comparison services and warning bulletins which we will be able to subscribe to at a small cost (or free, if we choose an advertising-supported service).

Ultimately, we are looking for economy both in cost and in how we use our time. The electronic shopping world will support this values shift as we move into a frictionless economy. E-commerce will likewise support our desire for economical and ecological solutions by its reduction of packaging through the visual representation of products and services in digital form. The resultant opportunity to use and reuse generic packaging will further reduce wasteful disposal as we strive to reach a better balance with our environment and use of the planet's resources. Special on-line services and auctions will further facilitate new ecologically-conscious systems of sharing, and will allow us to more easily recycle our unwanted things. In this new world we will carry less baggage and gain greater freedom from our lightened load.

These trends toward economy will also significantly alter the form of retailing, as shopping becomes more of an information-gathering exercise, as opposed to the industrial age physical shopping expedition. Retail will completely restructure and become a global game with new alliances formed to capture and serve world markets. The largest retailers will become vertically integrated and will own the manufacturing processes, on the one end, and home delivery systems on the other, with their old core service of merchandising and card payment systems existing in the middle. Other retailers will achieve the same result with alliances and selected suppliers.

All of these changes reflect our desire, as sovereign individuals, for greater degrees of personal expression and freedom in our choices of when and from where to engage in given activities, including shopping. The e-tailing environment will empower us and support our individual sovereignty as never before, and we will gain more personal time and a greater measure of control over our lives.

TRENDS AND IMPLICATIONS

Advertising and Marketing

* Customization of advertising is developing, based on tracking of user preferences. This will truly bring marketing to the one-to-one model. As a result, advertising will become relevant and will therefore be seen as the presentation of useful information.

* Retailers will move to pull marketing strategies through the anticipation of customer needs. In the new paradigm, marketers will present the information and the consumer will pull it towards them.

* Permission marketing will gain momentum. This genre of marketing includes newsletters, e-flyers, referrals, and the like, in which there is a voluntary participation of subscription by the individual.

Consumer Purchasing

* New buying services and on-line auctions will create an easier buying environment. New product comparison services will allow us to move from decisions to informed choices in our buying.

* Mass consumerism and shopping for the sake of shopping is on the decline, in favor of informed, judicious buying.

* The art of buying well will reach new heights via the networked economy. Pricing will become incredibly sharp due to global competition among retailers and auction services.

* The new services will allow us to acquire and divest ourselves of things more easily and lead less cluttered lives. We will move to ecological living as we recycle more things. New reconditioning services will spring up, as the value of used goods increases. As the reuse and recycling of products improves through the e-commerce world, residual value will become an important factor in the purchase decision, driving quality and longevity trends in product manufacturing.

* New sharing communities or clubs will develop around the sharing and pooling of items which we do not need to own on a one-to-one basis.

Technology Drivers

* Digital services will lead the way in moving to e-commerce. Financial services, music and video are first in line, and other high-value services such as travel, entertainment ticketing and automotive services will be early followers.

* Global alliances of retailers will form, facilitating on-line shopping in other countries.

✳ Microchip card technology will enable the micro financial transaction on the Internet. This will lead to the introduction of a range of services priced in the cents to a dollar range, to help us buy and sell products, services and information. This, in turn, will further fuel the e-commerce world.

Retail Transformation Themes

✳ "Bricks and mortar" department store retail will become entertainment based (in that it will need to be entertaining to capture our interest) and mass merchants of commodities will transform to electronic ordering, with personal delivery or personal pick-up.

✳ We will see the advent of shopping basket analysis and price comparison services and personalized systems for tracking of our personal inventories.

✳ We will enter the world of a frictionless economy as the distance between manufacturer and buyer narrows. Unnecessary layers of distribution and transshipment will be removed from the process to yield lower prices and greater efficiency in the marketplace.

✳ The role of the retailer will change. Some will only survive as portals. Large retailers will move to vertical integration and will own everything from the manu-facturing process through to home delivery services.

✳ Major malls will alter to become entertainment centers offering a plethora of dining options, theaters, thrill rides and unique gathering places. They will also serve as pick-up depots for electronic orders. Major malls that don't transform will fail.

The Customer Relationship

✴ Retailers will shift the emphasis of their marketing from promotion to long term loyalty as margins thin out and discounting becomes an everyday occasion. Relationship programs will encompass the entire lifetime experience of the customer.

✴ New truth in advertising is emerging as a manifestation of the spiritual value of honesty, guided by the court of public opinion.

✴ The total customer interface will take on new levels of importance and will include relevance of product, timing of presentation, ease of shopping, fulfillment time, quality of goods and services, guarantees, delivery flexibility and care and ease of return.

CHAPTER FIVE

A Growing Culture of Service

The idea of being of service to others and to all of life is gaining pervasive acceptance as we mature as a society. This is an important shift away from the existing focus on self which peaked in the late 1980s. In Western society, the self-centered ego consciousness of the industrial age is waning. We are seeing the rise of an increasing focus on service which is changing not only the way we do business, but the way we interact with our loved ones and the world at large. Two key factors in this shift can be found in (a) the new one-to-one marketing strategies, which focus on meeting the customer's needs, and (b) the adoption of Spiritual Values by a growing number of people as they move toward individual sovereignty and experience a resultant desire to extend themselves to others. Both of these changes have contributed to turning our attention away from ourselves. The ultimate result is a genuine and pervading, heart-felt sense of giving in both our personal and business lives.

Voluntarily Giving of Ourselves

As we make the shift to a Spiritual Values based structure we are seeing this expressed in our increasing interest in assisting others. In many societies, the old adage that it is better to give than to receive seems to have taken hold, and the shift in the direction of serving others is taking on mass proportions in the form of volunteerism. Charitable giving is also on the increase as part of the shift to a Spiritual Values driven world. Now more than ever we are reaching out to help others who are in need. The search for our true identity and desire to express ourselves in unique ways—through our choices of work, leisure and charitable giving activities—also means that the choice of charitable causes to become involved in is expanding as support levels increase.

Many people are finding that these giving activities are allowing them to experience a new joy and freedom in their lives. In essence, they are learning that we are all unique beings, each of us on a personal journey, and that we are here to learn from one another. When we can help another, it brings us joy and fulfillment we cannot possibly feel in any other way.

The Psychology of Giving

If you have ever felt frustrated, angry or even depressed, and then had the experience of completely forgetting these feelings because someone else needed your help and you responded to the need, then you have felt the power of giving. By giving of ourselves, our own cares are somehow diminished or put into proper perspective. In such circumstances, where we take our attention off ourselves and place our focus on helping or giving to another, we are quickly pulled out of the negative spiral of emotions. In fact, the placing of undue amounts of attention on the self (turning inward/introversion) is actually the cause of many of our diseases and social problems. But, by giving, people in this situation can turn the energy around and bring self-worth and joy back into their lives.

When we approach any situation with a view to how we can help, we are invoking a powerful spiritual principle. If we can relate to those around us from a service perspective, we will reap the positive benefits because we are not just doing, but giving to or serving another. This same principle holds opportunity for organizations. If organizations can shift from being solely focused inwardly on profits, and begin to focus outwardly on serving, they will create a shift in energy that is genuinely felt by the customer. In the end, this will actually lead to greater profits.

Marketing Focuses on the Customer

This service principle can be seen at work in the new focus on the customer, which is changing traditional marketing approaches in favor of strategies that actually consider and meet the individual customer's needs. This should be good news to all, because we know what it is like to be a customer. Certainly, the trend to a service culture would seem to indicate that one thing we do not want is to be processed en masse. To date, publishing and electronic media have responded well to this fact with a plethora of options, and marketing has likewise responded with a shift from push to pull techniques, as it increasingly addresses the market of one, the individual. As discussed in chapter four, the new e-commerce technology is enabling the marketing sector to make this shift and to identify, focus on and address the individual customer's needs.

This is a far cry from the old marketing model, which was a push strategy whereby products were marketed and pushed at the consumer. In the new millennium, however, the old 4 P's of marketing of the industrial age (product, price, place and promotion) are giving way to a new customer centered approach and a shift to pull marketing. This means designing programs that cause the customer to pull the product or service into their own orbit rather than the marketer trying to push it into the hands of the consumer. Marketers refer to the new system as the 4 C's of marketing: customer need, cost, convenience and communication—four main factors which customers are seeking. In some cases, when a wholesaler or other distributor is a key factor, a 5th C is added: compensation. The customer, however, remains at the center of the new marketing system and the ability to tailor marketing to the individual will continue to build new expectations in customer service and relations.

Restructuring Around a Service Principle

Since most organizations are serving customers of some kind, they also recognize that public expectations of service are dramatically changing. As a society, we defined success in the late 20th century in financial terms. But in the new millennium we are shifting to a new value set. Many of us are already discovering that money does not necessarily bring happiness. We are discovering that what truly motivates us is how we feel. Success in the new era will therefore be measured in terms of how people feel about their lives, not how much money they earn.

With this emerging realization that it is the feeling that counts, customers are increasingly expecting more from the service providers they choose. In short, they expect to feel good about their dealings with a company or organization and the way that they are treated by that company. The key to success lies in meeting or surpassing those expectations.

The old familiar saying, "The customer is always right," is a very basic articulation of the need for a service consciousness that many companies have recognized. In fact, numerous companies have created successful core ideologies around a service consciousness, as explored in chapter seven. Their service ideology is then reflected in a motto or mission statement. Still, restructuring an organization around this principle will be new to many organizations and may challenge those that are product or process driven at the present. This shift will be necessary, for ultimate performance and competitiveness.

In an organization where the focus is on service, the benefit is that everybody wins. The organization functions better and is more efficient in its interaction, and the customer actually feels the difference. The men and women who make up the organization also win because the result is a work environment based on Spiritual Values. Their reward is the job satisfaction that comes from working in a productive, creative and growing environment. The organization becomes a more relaxed, positive and fun place to work, which allows it to attract top quality staff who, in turn, create higher levels of service in the organization. The overall result is an organization that becomes more profitable through customer sales and increased corporate productivity.

Creating a Genuine Service Consciousness

In order to win in the new service oriented economy, the goal of leading organizations will be to offer this genuine from-the-heart level of service. If an organization can create this model of service and exude an attitude of helpfulness and teamwork, then it will also be able to service its customers with the same genuine attitude, and the difference will be felt.

The question then becomes how best to foster such an attitude of service in an organization. The answer lies in the fact that an organization, like a physical body, is as good as the sum, health or level of awareness of its cells or various parts. In other words, a company's quality of service is ultimately a direct reflection of the qualities inherent in the individuals who are providing the service. For example, if I am a kind, forgiving, respectful person, I will project that set of values in my work as well as in my personal relationships. This will, in turn, affect and determine the service levels of any organization in which I work.

In many respects, the degree to which a person incorporates Spiritual Values into their life determines their consciousness and approach to life. The level of consciousness of a company is therefore the result of the Spiritual Values held by the individuals who work there. Encouraging the development of these Spiritual Values in its employees is therefore a very healthy thing for any organization to do. When individuals grow spiritually, they have improved self-worth, greater creativity, and a feeling of harmony or balance. Other performance improvement factors include a higher degree of responsibility and teamwork and increased team spirit. All of these attributes contribute to greater efficiency and overall performance. Ultimately, the staff is more productive and the organization is able to accomplish more with fewer resources.

The enlightened organization of the new millennium will actually be fostering the adoption of Spiritual Values by its employees and these new values will bring a new set of behaviors that will lead to higher profitability. As the individuals within the company are given an opportunity to express themselves and take on greater responsibility, they will become different people, better people in that they will be more self-assured, relaxed, and confident and have a greater sense of self worth and an increased sense of humor. These are the kinds of people others like to work amongst and be with.

In short, in the shift to becoming Spiritual Values driven, organizational changes will actually be fostering a transformation of the individuals in the organization. We can look for this trend to take on mass proportions in the next ten years, ultimately improving countless organizations and the quality of service they are able to provide. As a part of this shift, the customers of these organizations will be served from the new platform of Spiritual Values. Reciprocally, customers will respond positively to these organizations and reward them with their business. After all, who does not want to be treated with respect and a genuine caring attitude that is delivered from the heart?

Organizations Foster Spiritual Values in Employees

This empowerment of the individual does not affect only the workplace, but extends to our home lives as well, and how we love and care for one another is now beginning to reflect this attitude of serving others. Generally, we are more demonstrative of affection. We can now hug friends, male and female alike, more openly and can feel comfortable expressing love to them as well. We are also learning how to express divine love by sharing our feelings with one another. Specifically, we are learning how to talk about how we feel and, at the same time, we are beginning to care more about other people and how they feel. This theme of giving in relationships is moving us to a greater degree of freedom where we can have our own unique interests and still share other interests with our partner. In learning how to respect our partners' space, we can more easily accept whatever personal agendas they may have, and allow them to learn from life in their own way and at their own pace. These changes will continue to evolve and, as we grow spiritually as individuals, we will increasingly seek ways to be of service and giving to our loved ones.

The Art of Listening

One of the most important and unique ways we can serve those we care about, as well as those we wish to assist, is simply by listening. Indeed, listening is an art form which we will be increasingly developing and applying in our personal lives, our volunteer work and on the job. This unique way to serve another will also become a powerful new business tool, which enables leaders to pool talent and ideas and become harvesters of ideas, as discussed in chapter seven. As individuals, we will also benefit from our interaction in this way, and our creativity and ability to handle life's little problems will increase as we move outside of our traditional problem solving modes and seek solutions to our challenges by listening to others and to life itself.

SYNOPSIS

As we proceed into the new millennium, we will be moving consistently away from the self-indulgent lifestyle of the last years of the 20th century. The result will be a genuine and heart-felt sense of giving and a desire to be of service, the ripple effects of which will take on a myriad of forms. What we are witnessing is the development of a culture of service which will ultimately affect our relationships and social interaction, our expectations of service from the service providers we choose (and ultimately from the government as well), and, of course, the way that organizations conduct business.

This service culture is being reflected in a growing focus on the customer, both in marketing and in business. In fact, organizations will increasingly structure around customer service. In many cases, this new focus on the customer will involve giving members of the organization the opportunity to grow, to actually

64

change in consciousness, so that they can evolve to a whole new way of being. Indeed, it is beneficial to encourage individuals and business structures to think in terms of "what can I give" and "what can I learn" with each interaction. This way, the customer wins, the employee wins and the organization wins as well.

In reality, the new 21st century workplace will give us an opportunity to live our newfound spiritual awareness. It will allow us to grow spiritually and will foster a greater adoption of Spiritual Values, on the job and in our personal lives. These values include respect for others and all life, responsibility, and an appreciation for working in harmony as team players on the greater team of humanity. Look for this shift as an essential ingredient in successful organizations in the new millennium.

TRENDS AND IMPLICATIONS

Voluntary Giving
* As we evolve to greater levels of self-confidence and greater self-worth, we are also shifting to outer focused (as opposed to self-centered) lifestyles. A new level of attention is being placed on being of service and giving to others. Volunteerism and charitable giving are on the rise, with a multitude of causes available to support. Support of specific charity organizations reflects our increased desire to express our uniqueness as sovereign individuals.

Service Marketing
* A focus on service to the customer is reflected in new thinking and the resultant marketing systems that are being and will continue to be built around the customer, by creating and selling to needs. New targeting in the one-to-one era will enable customer offers to be

presented as timely and relevant to individual customer needs

✳ Increased expectations of customer service created by the new one-on-one marketing will ultimately affect our expectations of government services as well. In response, public service will eventually become just that: service. Just as companies are now able to cater to the "market of one", our public services will eventually follow.

✳ Marketing will serve the customer by shifting to pull rather than push techniques. Industrial age push marketing (the 4 P's) will be replaced with the 4C's, which place the attention once again on the customer.

The New Service Consciousness

✳ Success is increasingly being defined in terms of how we feel about our lives, rather than in monetary or financial terms. This leads to greater expectations of customer service, since we want to feel good about our dealings with a given company or service provider.

✳ Enlightened organizations of the new millennium will actually seek to foster individual development and the adoption of Spiritual Values in their employees. When the consciousness of employees change, the organization will also change. A more relaxed self-confident at-work lifestyle creates a more receptive environment for serving others, because attention shifts away from a focus on the self, towards a greater caring for others.

✳ We will increasingly seek ways to be of service to our loved ones, in our personal relationships.

✳ The art of listening will be developed as a unique way to serve another and will become a powerful new business tool, which enables leaders to pool talent and ideas and become harvesters of ideas.

CHAPTER SIX

The Redefinition of Institutions

As we begin the new millennium, our social institutions are undergoing significant changes and our changing values are really at the root of it all. In actuality, our institutions are making a transition to better serving the individual. This transition is being fueled by various factors, including our desire to take more responsibility for our lives, our changing perceptions and expectations of service, and our ecological/economical interest in minimizing the use of resources. All of these factors are combining to create changes that will inevitably affect our governmental, legal, health and educational institutions, as well as organized religion. As society changes consciousness, our societal institutions will follow suit.

Understanding the Cause of the Changes

Basically, as we begin the shift to the "age of the individual", the "communications age" or the "networked economy", the industrial-age institutional models are no longer working. These institutions were born out of the era of mass production, when economies of scale were found in the manufacture of services on a large scale. Today, however, as people in increasing numbers are taking responsibility for their lives, our expectations of service are also changing. We want control and are no longer willing to blindly trust a system or an institution. This movement will grow with the trend moving toward greater input and responsiveness to specific individual, not mass, needs.

Spiritual Values are also trending towards ecology/economy in that we are looking for the most efficient way for our public institutions to deliver a service, and we will see these values and the Spiritual value of service reflected in the coming changes to our institutions. As the trend to serving others increases, and as we give to others as a way of life, we will want to be treated with this same caring and responsive approach. This shift is also leading to expectations of service on our terms, which means we will expect service when we want it, where we want it and how we want it. This expectation is being met in the business world via e-commerce and the new just-in-time information services, and our public service institutions will eventually follow suit and be required to respond to public need as well.

Taking Responsibility for our Health

All of the factors discussed above play a significant role in many of the changes that we are now seeing in our medical institutions and the services they offer. This is particularly so in heavily regulated jurisdictions. The trend today is toward the development of specialty service facilities that provide care specific to the needs of patients. In keeping with the new Spiritual Values and the principle of economy discussed in chapter 12, we will not want services we do not need. This shift, which will accelerate in the coming years, is a movement toward services geared for smaller and smaller groups of people and toward a better ability to meet the specialized needs of individuals. For instance, many women no longer feel comfortable giving birth in a place for healing the sick and are seeking viable alternatives. In many cases, geriatric care can also be provided in self-aided environments and valuable hospital resources are not needed for many elderly, who only require some help some of the time.

We are also recognizing, in increasing numbers, that we, not our doctors, are responsible for our healing and health. Previously, the problem was viewed as outside of our responsibility and control. The allopathic medicines and practice run in tandem with this old consciousness in which people expected the doctor to just fix them. However, there is a growing shift in the direction of understanding that we are responsible for our condition and that we will gain the most spiritually by taking an active role in our healing.

In response to this shift, alternative and natural therapies are now emerging as mainstream options that we can choose in bringing ourselves back to a state of healthy balance. A greater understanding also exists of our connection with the whole of creation and the energy that works through and sustains all of us. This recognition is part of society's change in consciousness, which is allowing us to see imbalance in our energy (body, mind and spirit) as a root cause of "dis-ease." The new therapies are emerging to assist us in solving our own problems, as we increasingly take responsibility for our own health. In the new millennium, more and more people will understand that healing is actually a change in consciousness and a realization and treatment of cause of the disease (dis-ease), rather than just the effects.

Religion for the Individual

There have also been major changes in many of our traditional belief systems. In some cases the established religions, which have been built on centuries of dogma, are serving only their own needs and are not able to serve their adherents in understanding truth in today's world. They are simply too rigid to change fast enough to maintain relevance. Today, these old religions are breaking down into smaller units as people search for spiritual guidance that has greater relevance to their lives, and numerous new belief systems and religions are forming in response to our quest for truth. As an example, we are seeing many more branches of Christianity than existed a hundred years ago, and even individual congregations are breaking away and forming their own unique form of worship.

Eventually, more individuals will begin taking responsibility for their own spiritual development, rather than placing it in the hands of a religious institution that is full of practices that are irrelevant to our current thirst for truth. And, just as we are moving to a market-of-one in our access to customized goods and services, we will move towards an individual market-of-one in belief systems. More individuals will then seek out support systems that help them discover their own truth from within. These support systems include personal growth and development seminars, yoga, specialized healing such as Reiki, meditation and self-help groups.

Government and the Quest for Freedom

Meanwhile, in the secular world, our expectations of government are also shifting and our overall need for government services is in decline as we opt for taking greater responsibility for our lives. As a society, we are asking for less service and more control. Again, the new ecological consciousness means that we do not want services we do not need. We will increasingly become willing to pay only for what we use. The use of toll roads, which are prevalent in the United States and are now appearing in other Western countries, is one sign of the already expanding user-pay philosophy. This trend will continue and will eventually be reflected in a shift to consumption taxes and in new efficiencies in service, which will be discovered to help reduce overall taxation. Our access to information and the flexibility of consumption taxation will dramatically improve our ability to make personal choices in the new millennium and, in the not-too-distant future, we will choose the mix of ingredients we require and desire in creating our lives.

One result of these changes will be seen in a less protective legislative environment which will be provided in many jurisdictions for two reasons. First, as our values evolve to a better understanding of our spiritual roots and we become more spiritual, we will need fewer rules to govern our behavior. We will naturally do what is right, because we will have a better understanding of the law of cause and effect and the fact that what we give out, we will certainly get back at some point in time.

Second, we will want greater freedom from the restrictive nature of regulation. As individuals, we will operate from a higher ethical viewpoint and will want to create our lives with as few restrictions as possible. Accordingly, as we move to the adoption of Spiritual Values, we will feel a need for fewer consumer and social laws to protect us. At the same time, we will also be dealing with service providers around the world, who are outside of the reach and ability of our home government to protect us, and therefore render such protection obsolete.

71

Ultimately, I believe that the ethics of service providers and product producers will also be elevated and, as a result, our need for consumer protection will further diminish. This will be accelerated and facilitated by the ease and speed of information sharing in the networked economy. In other words, the new information-based economy will essentially be self-policing, since the court of public opinion and reaction will be swift and inevitable.

This will also lead to a growing focus on the ethics of companies, with ethics becoming a major decision-making factor in our purchase of products and services. Ethical mutual funds are an early sign of this trend. As consumers, we are looking increasingly for corporate accountability in the new millennium. The day of the faceless corporation is gone and leaders are now required to be visibly up front with the practices and policies of their corporation. The single protester is now a reality and just one voice can change the practices of a corporation in the new electronic age.

Our view of censorship will change as well, since the authorities will no longer be able to control information of any kind. As an open forum of opinion and information, the Internet can only be self-policed. We will have access to any information and so truth in all corporate, governmental and institutional activities, and in the behavior of public figures, will be the only way to operate in the open world of information that is unfolding for us.

Education Shifts to Serving the Student

The Internet and the new age of information have particular significance in the realm of education, and we are seeing our educational institutions undergoing great changes, as well. Our young people have been born into the new consciousness and will be responsible for leading this shift to the new Spiritual Values driven economy, which is the greatest shift in history in the way we operate as human beings. Their educational system needs to reflect the freedom they will require in order to create productive and responsible lives for themselves in this new world.

Many schools, however, are still being run on the old industrial-age model, which is very much akin to the old marketing push system. In other words, as was the case for many of us when we went to school, information is being pushed at students and in some cases stuffed down their throats. Many of us recall being forced to agree with everything in our text books and to assume that, if it was in a book, it must be true.

This type of mass processing of individuals simply does not work any longer, as the current drop out rates clearly attest. In fact, students often feel like caged animals in these industrial-age educational institutions. Even the expectations we hold as parents will no longer work for our children. The jobs we trained for will no longer exist and the rules of interaction have definitely changed. Our children will go far beyond our vision of what is possible. Therefore, our vision of what a child should do or learn must also change. What they need is to be served on their terms and in ways that will actually benefit them. After all, they are creating their lives for themselves and no one else. They will intuitively know what they need and want.

Students of today are responding best to the pull system verses the push system of the industrial age. This means that, rather than having information pushed at them, these young people need to be prepared for the just-in-time world they will be entering. They will need to know how to retrieve and work with information, not just memorize it. With increasingly direct access to any information, they can then simply retrieve information as they need it. We call this just-in-time information.

Our children are already learning how to manage vast quantities of information and how to access it, and consequently do not suffer from the information overload experienced by older generations. They are also learning early the value of working together in teams. After all, no one has all the answers. In this way, they are again being prepared for the consciousness that exists in the world they will be entering as young adults.

Other positive changes that we are seeing include the fact that students are beginning to be given a greater choice of subjects and more flexibility on how they complete assignments. Personal creativity is an important ingredient, which is being increasingly acknowledged. It is also significant that our children will be accessing information from the same primary sources we use, in preparing their school assignments. As a result, they will be enabled to form their own opinions, rather than simply repeating those of other authors.

The age of the sovereign individual will be ushered in with the current wave of young people functioning as an integral part of the millennium shift, and they will have a dramatic effect on our social institutions. They expect freedom to express themselves and to create their lives in their own way. Their attitudes and expectations will contribute greatly to the creation or instigation of changes on a global basis, and the networked world will facilitate this change.

SYNOPSIS

As our values shift and we change, basic services in our societies must also shift to be in tune with the new consciousness. As evolving individuals, we are becoming more aware of our spiritual heritage and we are taking greater responsibility for our lives. The need to be responsible for our lives will lead to greater input in how our institutions are run and will be reflected in our desire for ecological economy in how much help we ask for and how we decide to help ourselves.

Ecology is a strong spiritual theme of this shift, as we move to the new values platform that causes us to use as few resources as possible and to be in harmony with the earth and others. This trend toward ecology will lead to major changes, with a new economy of service use and an economy of service delivery on the part of our institutions. The overall need for service will also decrease as we take more responsibility for our lives. As an example, consumer protection will not be as necessary in the new Spiritual Values driven, e-commerce enabled world.

The value of service to others will also be reflected in our expectations of service levels. As the world continues to move toward the market of one, certain institutions will likewise move gradually to personalized service, with the help of systems and the Internet. Other institutions will decline as their relevance to our lives diminishes.

These dramatic shifts in values will ultimately ripple out to affect all of our institutions, not the least of which is our educational system, preparing our youth for the new world they will enter. In advanced educational settings, children are now learning how to pull information out of the system and the most successful educational systems in the new millennium will work with this principle.

The current young generation is in tune with the new technology, the enabler of the shift to the "sovereign" empowered individual. As they mature, they will lead the transition to the new networked economy and will be responsible for many of the institutional changes required by the increasing adoption of Spiritual Values. These youth will require freedom to create and to express themselves, as they naturally seek to take responsibility for their own health and increasingly seek their own inner answers and spiritual understandings in life. It is for them that we are laying a new foundation, and they will build upon it boldly.

TRENDS AND IMPLICATIONS

* Mass production of the industrial age is shifting to personal service in the age of the individual. Key factors driving this change include technology, combined with the need for greater control over our lives and our changing expectations of service that are being created by the one-to-one consumer trends.
* We are no longer willing to simply trust in and rely upon a system. As we assume greater responsibility, we want greater input.

Medical Services

* The mass approach is no longer meeting personal needs. For example, geriatric and maternity services are no longer thought of as part of a hospital get well environment. We are moving toward specialty facilities to meet individual needs.
* We are beginning to take greater responsibility for our own health and healing. Healing will be no longer something outside of ourselves but as something within our ability to manage. We will also begin to understand

"dis-ease" as a state of imbalance and to seek causes within our control. As we progress into the new world, there will be a realization at the societal level that a healing is a change in consciousness and that the conditions that we created or accepted are at the root of our disease.

* Natural and alternatives therapies will become mainstream.

Religions

* Old established religions will continue their break down into smaller units.

* Many new teachings will continue to emerge to fill the need for greater truth and understanding.

* Spirituality is moving to the mass market of one, just as in the marketing of products. New teachings will help us discover our own individual truth from within, and will provide tools that anyone can use in this unique discovery process.

Government

* We are seeking less service and more personal control as we accept greater responsibility. We will be seeking more freedom to create our lives, through support of action like free trade.

* Less consumer protection will be required as the networked economy quickly communicates unethical services through open forums that provide instant feedback to providers.

* Fewer laws will be wanted or required as we seek greater freedom of action and the global arena creates the need for a level playing field of taxation with less regulation.

✳ The move to user pay services will accelerate, to reduce taxes and to assist in competing in the global economy.

✳ We are entering a self-regulated world and information distribution will no longer be in the control of governments.

✳ With the decline of censorship, the new skill of discrimination will be taught to our children

Business

✳ A new level of ethics is emerging in business. The organization is no longer a faceless entity.

✳ Business contracts will be win-win deals to foster longevity of the relationship.

✳ Ethics of companies is becoming a major factor in consumer purchasing decisions (e.g. ethical mutual funds, Body Shop, Roots).

Education

✳ Mass processing of students is no longer working, as witnessed by current drop out rates, frustration and even crime.

✳ Education will move from the push system to the pull system and will consequently deliver a better educational experience, at less cost. Just-in-time information is a theme of the new age and today's students will learn it in school. There will be no need to memorize. Instead, students will be taught to pull the information they need from the network.

✳ Students will work in teams to complete assignments, as in the future work environment they will be entering.

✳ Personal creativity will be a key ingredient in the new educational model. New computer-aided education will allow global sharing of learning systems and best practices. This will create a more personal learning environment attuned to the needs and pace of each student and will save significant resources.

CHAPTER SEVEN

Catching The Wave In The Workplace

The general consciousness of the world is changing as we make the transition to a networked economy and a growing portion of the population embraces the new Spiritual Values. This shift has both created a new understanding of wealth (to be explored in chapter eleven) and given rise to an increasing focus on service, which is having a significant effect on the way we do business. As a result, many systems in our society, along with our businesses, companies and organizations, are experiencing a corresponding shift. It stands to reason, then, that by understanding these new values and forces, and by working with the flow of this change, we can begin to build better lives and better organizations, organizations that are more responsive to the customer or service franchise.

New Structures Are Fostering Spiritual Values

Leading edge organizations are restructuring in two significant ways, both of which reflect the new Spiritual Values consciousness and the freedom gained in a networked economy. First, we are seeing a shift toward flatter organizational structures and, second, the traditional organization pyramid is being inverted. These two trends are having dramatic effects on the roles and responsibilities of staff and are contributing to the personal growth of employees as a result. The trend indicates that the new structures and the resultant changes will further support the adoption of Spiritual Values in thousands of organizations in the coming years.

Delayering the Organization Cultivates Responsibility

The first of the changes to take place within the last decade is the flattening of the traditional organizational structure. In many corporations, management has had to make the organization more cost effective in its delivery of goods or services to the customer. Structural flattening, which is a result of a delayering process started in the 1990s, ultimately reduces the number of levels of customer service between the CEO and the front line sales/service staff. The result is a much leaner organization, supported by technology, delivering the same or greater output.

In the newly flattened organization, each position has to pull its own weight. Every position counts. There is no room for extra staff and everyone on the team is counted upon to deliver his or her part. There is, as a result, a greater accountability and responsibility inherent in each position.

This concept of responsibility applies not only to our lives at work, but expands into our total lives. As we become more spiritually aware, we recognize that we are all on one team, that is, we are all part of the whole. Further, we begin to understand that we must take responsibility for our actions, thoughts, words and deeds. In essence, we are learning that we get back what we give out or, as the saying goes, "What comes around, goes around." The spiritual principle expressed by this saying is referred to as the principle of "cause and effect", which is described later.

In the new corporate consciousness of the 21st century, there is no more hiding behind others in the organization. We are becoming our own islands of action, rather than extensions of someone else's responsibility. As such, we are all like critical elements of a living organism. Each has a role or function to perform and each is necessary to the proper functioning of the whole. So, in the new millennium, each person will become a vital and integral part of the organization, a more meaningful part of the team.

Management is a Team

The team environment will be crucial to expanding business where a number of disciplines and multiple expertise are required to deliver a project or run a business unit. Old style competitive management structures simply will not succeed in the new world of razor sharp e-commerce competition. So, for many organizations with hierarchical structures (the military command model), the challenge will be how best to shift from this old industrial age model to a new model which better serves the customer.

In the industrial age, competition was a matter of size, and internal competition created healthy regeneration, but the old systems will not be able to react fast enough or be creative enough to succeed in the new economy. In this new millennium, the entire energy of the organization must combine with synergistic results to win. Teamwork is a major key as organizations flatten in the new frictionless economy. Silos will come down in organizations to foster the kind of creativity and team spirit necessary to win in the new marketplace.

The senior management of the 21st century industry leaders

will themselves be balanced people, in organizations driven by Spiritual Values. They will work as a team and help each other to a greater degree. This approach will be fostered down the line, and greater attention will be placed on having a helpful, caring attitude. Incentive programs that foster such an attitude will be a key to communicating the importance of team results.

Equality and Respect for All

This trend of flat organizational structures is also fostering a new respect for each employee for the role each performs and the contribution each makes. In the leaner, flattened organization, respect for each person, no matter what his or her role or station, creates the opportunity of ideas coming from any source. This in turn will open us up to listening as a way of operating in our daily activities. We can tap a greater pool of idea talent as a team. Ideas will be generated at a faster rate, as more people are included in and commit themselves to the process. Everyone will feel motivated and involved. This in turn creates greater fulfillment and productivity in the new 21st century organization. The work environment will change to a more supportive environment.

We will begin to see everyone around us as an equal regardless of rank, and we will learn to tap the creative process of the group and of ourselves. We are all creators and when we listen, we can hear a great deal of insight and creativity. The solutions are all around us. We only have to be willing to listen and understand that answers can come from any source. Those that become harvesters of ideas from the sources around them will find greater success with the input of their whole team in the coming years. No longer will any role be a single-minded effort in the new economy as this shift takes place in organizations.

Inverting the Pyramid & Building a Service Chain

The second restructuring trend involves an inversion of the typical organizational pyramid. The idea of service is important to understanding how this shift will come about since, in the new model, the advanced customer-service driven organizations will place the customer at the top of the pyramid and will recognize the relationship that each individual has with the customer. Successful organizations in the new millennium will think of each relationship as a point of service and each department will be defined in relation to the service it renders to the customer.

In reality, many people in typical organizations do not have direct customer contact. In the new model they will be defined as part of the customer service chain. When organizations are structured to serve the customer, each unit is identified as either serving the customer or as serving other units that serve the customer. Either way, they play a crucial role in what is, in effect, a chain of service. This service chain is not unlike the food chain. Every link is vital and has a valuable role to play, and it is important for each business unit, section or individual to know and clearly define which other units it serves. If each person can focus on serving others around them, they will actually be serving the customer albeit indirectly.

The following chart provides an example of an organizational structure in which each department takes on their role as one of service to other departments in the organization, thereby forging a strong chain of service to the customer.

The New Customer Service Model

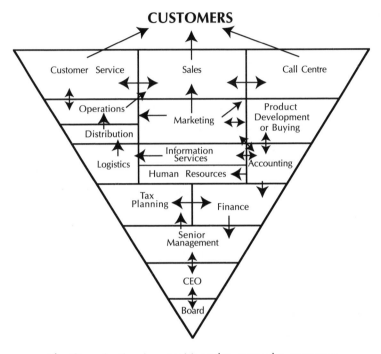

The Organization is repositioned to serve the customer
and each department knows its service role is supporting
other departments to serve the customer.

In such organizations, where the focus is on the customer
via a service chain, a genuine service culture is developed which
the customer cannot help but feel.

NOTE: This chart is for illustrative purposes and not meant to be
functionally correct for any particular organization.

The Empowerment of the Individual Employee

In many instances, technology is a part of the solution to better service levels. But advanced organizations at the leading edge of this shift are discovering that quality of service ultimately depends upon the quality of the interaction that customers have with the men and women who make up the service-providing organization. They have come to understand that there is an equation, "As within, so without." This simply means that the qualities inherent in the delivery of service are a direct result of the qualities and values of the people in the organization. When we identify the qualities we wish to project as an organization, we can see the importance of the values that our co-workers hold. Thus, the organization benefits in significant measure from creating a structure and environment in which its employees can grow. The enlightened organization of the new millennium will therefore actively seek ways to foster the adoption of Spiritual Values by its employees. These new values will bring a whole new set of behaviors, which will in turn lead to higher profitability for the company.

The New CEO

Of course, the shift to a Spiritual Values driven organization starts at the top. And a whole separate book could be written on how to lead an organization into the future based on the new Spiritual Values. For now, however, I offer a few specific keys that can assist the visionary leader in taking steps in this direction.

First, the CEO must believe that his people are there to do much more with their life than just earn money. This means understanding that the employees in the company need to grow in a balanced way by leading balanced lives. The successful CEO in the new millennium will foster balance in his people, and therefore in his organization.

Second, the new CEO will create a culture of service within their organization and will structure the organization to be attentive and respond quickly to customer needs. This will be a much easier task with employees who are happy, balanced and service oriented. However, the CEO must also have a solid vision of service that sets out what the corporation brings to the world and to its people. This requires determining what values the organization is to project: honesty, truth, compassion, humor, creativity, fairness, service, love, caring. These Spiritual Values will depend on the nature of the organization and its mission, but it is essential that the new leader have a vision of service in order to successfully lead the organization to greater success.

Leadership is a Vision of Service

History has born out the importance of positioning organizations to serve their employees, customers or the community, or all three, rather than simply focusing on profits. After all, our existence on Earth is about much more than just money. It is about our personal growth and about helping and giving to others. One mark of successful organizations today is that they have been guided over the years by a mission that held the value of service to others. One example of a successful corporation with a service-oriented mission that has carried it a long way is the Motorola company, with its statement: "The purpose of Motorola is to honorably service the community..." . Other such service-oriented mottoes include American Express declaration of "heroic customer service"; Ford's "People as the source of our strength"; and Merck's mission "to alleviate pain and disease." Of course, a true service consciousness goes far beyond a motto. The key ingredient is the communication and support of this mission, for the entire organization must be aligned with the mission, if it is to be attained. It must pervade the entire company, the very structure of the organization, and each employee.

Many leading corporations today have a mission statement that incorporates the concept of giving to the community, the world, or its employees. In the new century, more organizations will follow suit, creating mission statements that are focused on the larger purpose of the organization and its role in the greater community or the world. The corporate mission of successful corporations will be aligned with the values it wishes to project to its community and its people. The creation and active promotion of such a mission statement within the organization itself will be an essential element for companies wishing to shift and adapt in the new millennium.

SYNOPSIS

There are a number of significant changes which are having a combined effect on the direction in which modern organizations are heading as we proceed into the new millennium. These changes, which include the growing culture of service that is gaining momentum in our society, and an increasing focus on the welfare of our employees, are creating corresponding structural changes within many leading-edge organizations. The modern leaner organization of the new era will reflect the growing emphasis on service and will give us an opportunity to become more responsible. As a result, we will gain in freedom and job satisfaction and perform better as a result.

The changes must occur from the top down, however, and it is critical that the leader of a company be in tune with the wave of change and actively foster the adoption of Spiritual Values, both by the organization and its employees. This includes creating an environment in which the individual employee is respected and teamwork is enhanced. In such an environment, we can tap into a greater pool of talent and insight, as opposed to operating as islands of endeavor, the latter being a very limited way of functioning at work, home or at play. Therefore, leaders in the new millennium will have an opportunity to act as harvesters of ideas, who lead the way through a clearly articulated mission statement that entails the qualities to which the organization aspires and includes a vision of service which will take the company into the new millennium.

TRENDS AND IMPLICATIONS

The Delayering Process

* The organizational delayering process is creating less distance between the CEO and the customer. This flattening of the organization is creating a new degree of responsibility for every employee. Staff is being empowered to make decisions and new responsibility is infused into every position.

* The expert of one is disappearing as business complexity increases. We are seeing the emergence of teams, which are now needed to achieve new product introductions or to advance the business, as no one has the expertise to do it all.

* Team work, combined with greater responsibility, is leading to a new respect for each person/position. The old ego consciousness of the industrial age is in decline as reliance on team players increases.

✳ The trend will be to team players who help each other. They will foster teamwork down the line. This will be critical in a frictionless economy with razor thin margins, where no energy can be wasted on internal fighting or turf wars. Incentive programs will be designed to support teamwork.

✳ Organizational silos will disappear.

✳ Listening will become an increasingly important business tool in the coming decade, as we move toward the recognition that all employees are important contributors and can provide valuable input. There will be no need to pretend that any one person knows it all, because everyone knows that it is not true.

✳ As more people are included in the process of listening and contributing, ideas and solutions will be generated faster—just what is needed in the new faster-paced world.

The Creation of a Service Chain

✳ Many organizations will be redrawing their organization structures and inverting the traditional organizational pyramid to put customers on top.

✳ Each business unit will then revise their objectives to either directly serve the customer or to provide service to other departments, thereby serving the customer indirectly. This creates a service chain in which each unit is positioned as a vital link serving the customer.

✳ Departmental goals and budgets are aligned to place responsibility and control with the user of the services.

✳ Everyone gains in freedom with the responsibility accepted. This leads to greater balance individually as people are given an opportunity to grow.

✳ The result will be the emergence of Spiritual Values (such as trust, respect, harmony, patience, caring, serving, freedom, and more) in the at-work lifestyle.

Leadership and a Vision of Service

✳ The trend will be toward business leaders who understand the bigger mission of the organization and who realize that the company's outward face to the customer is a reflection of the inner state of the organization and the qualities inherent in its employees.

✳ Balance will be fostered both in the advanced organization itself and its employees, creating a new caring attitude.

✳ Corporate leaders will move to a greater understanding that the corporation exists for more than just profit (just as we as individuals are realizing that we exist to do more than just make and spend money).

✳ The importance of giving to the staff, the community or the world is already a key component and core value in the missions of many of the oldest, successful corporations. This focus will grow.

✳ The enlightened CEO in the new millennium will have and promote a clear vision of how their corporation gives service to the community and the world at large.

✳ Corporations will align their mission statements with the Spiritual Values they wish to embody/embrace.

CHAPTER EIGHT

Leaving The Rat Race, Slowing The Pace

Have you noticed how the pace of life has picked up? Life seems to be speeding up, or at least the pace of change has increased. True, we have better access to information than ever before, but the fact is that we often have too much information to integrate into our lives. So, how can we keep up? The answer is that we can't without burning out and so we must find ways to adjust.

Towards a Creative Style of Living

Millions of people are discovering that it is actually necessary to slow down in order to live a balanced life in this fast-paced world. For many, however, this feels wrong, contrary as it is to the learned behavior of the industrial age. But, like skiers who must lean farther forward on a steeper hill to gain better control—a seemingly contrary action to the outside observer—we will, in significant numbers, be learning how to slow down as we move into the new Spiritual Values driven world.

At first, we may feel there is a lot that we will miss or that will not get done. However, by slowing down, we can and will actually become more productive, and will enjoy reaching our goals at the same time! This is possible because, when we slow down, we allow our creativity to play through. And by giving ourselves creative space or breathing room, we are able to see new solutions to difficulties and get ideas about our everyday challenges that might not have otherwise come to our attention if we were moving at the speed of light on the treadmill of life. When we slow down we can pay more attention to those around us, become better listeners and, consequently, avail ourselves of their wisdom as well. We become harvesters of ideas, but we must first make the time. And more and more of us will do so, as we progress into the age of the individual.

A New Trust and Respect for All

Ironically, the new age of the individual is reflected in the trend toward working in teams. Twenty years ago, the phenomenon of the single expert was a common reality, with much of the knowledge of a business being held by one person. Today, however, the pace of change has made this impossible. There is simply too much information to absorb, and projects are far more complex in today's systems-driven world than ever before. Now, organizations accomplish major objectives through teamwork, with project teams often coming together for a particular assignment and then disbanding once the project has been completed.

As we better understand the shift to the new economy, we can see the new values emerging in this concept of teamwork. Everyone is gaining in responsibility as organizations move toward a greater reliance on each individual to carry their own weight. We then begin to trust others to assist us and, as a result, we respect all individuals for their unique contribution.

The Personalization of Media

Information overload remains a fact of life that daily presents us with a multitude of choices. Do we read everything that comes to our door or across our desk, or do we exercise discrimination? The new millennium is about making choices from a broad selection of options. The question is how best to make those choices. As a first step, we can regain some of our own mental space by tuning out the media.

Everyday, the media bombards us with its view of the world and far too many people are allowing the media to define their universe. I am not saying that the media is bad, but the media-created world can present us with a very distorted view of reality, as reporters use every sound bite and gesture to create a newsworthy story that will grab enough attention to move the ratings up a notch or two. The result is a repetitious dissemination of news stories (as the media defines their reporting of events) some hyped beyond reason. As a result, many people are turning away from such news. This trend will be accelerated as part of the shift, with media saturation being replaced by a selective pulling of information by the public, as we progress into the world of just-in-time information. In other words, rather than allowing the media to push news at us by constantly watching and listening to mass media, we will begin to pull the information we require towards us from selected primary sources and on selected topics of our own choice.

In response, news will change as a product in the new millennium. We will increasingly be interested only in the facts and, when we want commentary, we will go to our chosen sources. We will begin to address ourselves to fact-based reports from original sources, which will be provided through service bureaus that present information based on our customized requirements. Analyses will be provided via other sources which will be easily purchased and downloaded, and news stories will be presented more like entertainment is today, segmented and offered in shows on particular interests such as world politics, global weather, areas of conflicts, crime stories, etc. This trend is seen now in its initial development stage, in the crime-stopper programs, rescue dramas, and news magazines that are gaining popularity. The networked economy will enable this just-in-time information and analysis in the early years of the new decade and the frenetic news-hyped world will come increasingly under our control in the new millennium.

The Decline of Multi-tasking

Another trend, both at work and in our lives, will be the movement away from multi-tasking, which, in the end, will prove to be less effective than focus. In fact, multi-tasking is a recipe for burnout which works counter to creative principles. In the new era, the creative approach will win out as we begin to collaborate with others more and focus on only the important agendas. Many have already learned that they can begin to slow the pace down by removing a single agenda item from each day, just one thing their day can do without. In the future we will extend this by asking ourselves, "What are the most important things I can do today to succeed?" The rest will wait. We will even learn to leave meetings when we can no longer serve the agenda, in order to make better use of our time.

In the end, we will be more effective and productive by doing less, because the things we actually do will be the vital tasks which move our agendas forward and accomplish our goals. This trend will evolve through various stages as we slow down more and more, as set out in the following chart.

TODAY	TOMORROW
Multi-tasking ➤ Split attention ➤ Slowing ➤ Taking items off agenda ➤ **Focus**	

Eventually, in just the opposite of the multi-task environment, we will create space in our day for contemplation of issues and opportunities and for reflection that fosters creative thought.

Living in the Moment

We will learn that being focused in the moment is the most productive and contented way to be. In fact, "living in the moment" appeared as one of the items on Chatelaine Magazine's "What We'll Take Checklist" of things women should take with them into the year 2000, along with such items as handwritten letters and fresh air, two other indicators of a more sanely-paced life.

When our attention is placed too far into the future, we feel stress as a result of fear about how things turn out. On the other hand, if we are focused on the past, with undue attention placed on events that have already transpired, we often waste time with feelings of regret. The truth is that the past cannot be changed and the future is not yet manifested. All opportunity therefore rests in the present. For this reason, it is best to place the greater part of our attention on the present, to live in the moment and be content with our lives, right now.

The Discovery of Simplicity

In a word, the above changes in both personal and work lives reflect a shift toward simplicity. Indeed, there is a strong trend towards simplification of our lives already evident today. Some are calling it "cashing out"; I call it "voluntary simplicity" and it has thousands of people moving to quieter settings, cottages or the country, while others are scaling back to live in simpler homes, condos or apartments. In many cases, the idea of living in a small city apartment and owning a place in the country is testimony to our changing perception of what is important in our lives. With this shift comes a focus on quality rather than quantity. So, while we may choose to have less in our closets, each item will likely reflect a quality choice. Both of these concepts of voluntary simplicity and quality over quantity are an extension of the ecology discussion, in chapter nine.

The Spiritual Values of joy and harmony, both with one's self and one's environment, are important themes which will gather momentum in the new millennium.

Those who will make a transition to a simpler life will be following their inner agendas, not the social agenda demanded by the media or environment. They will leave the world of social conformity and reinvent their lives by doing what brings them joy. In this transition, the pursuit of money will shift to second place. Seeking fulfillment through inner rather than outer circumstances will then lead to a return to simple pleasures. And so, as opposed to the disco frenzy of the 80s and 90s—when we were always on the go, dining out and socializing with others—we will move toward creating and protecting our personal time and enjoying simple pleasures such as reading, crafts and computer activities.

Surrendering Outcomes: Reducing Stress

This whole trend toward simplification and slowing down invokes the Principle of Reversed Effort (see chapter 12) and is, in part, about letting go of outcomes. This is also one of the key secrets to reducing our stress levels and living a more balanced and contented life, regardless of our circumstances.

As we grow in consciousness and accept the new awareness of ourselves as Spiritual beings having a human experience, we will begin to understand that we are not in control as an outer being. Our inner being actually has the last word. Outwardly, we have the responsibility of creating our lives through what we set in motion, but what comes of that creativity is up to our true self, Soul, and the Creator. We will come to understand that it is best to remain open to how things we set in motion actually manifest in our world. This is particularly so because, in our day to day lives, we actually lack the knowledge of what is for our greatest good, and the good of the whole, at the highest level. However, our inner being, Soul, knows.

Turning outcomes over to our inner side can be incredibly freeing. Some teachings call this step "surrender", meaning a surrender to the inner self or to the Creator. We are able to take this step once we reach the understanding that we cannot force an outcome. Then, we can let go and just enjoy the ride, so to speak.

Today, most of us are focused on the destination, rushing from place to place but observing very little in our travels between points. Yet, when we view life as a series of destinations connected by journeys in between, we will begin to see each journey as being just as important as the destination. We will learn more and more to stop and smell the roses as we realize that half the fun is getting there! In the new millennium, more and more of us will discover this principle and learn to integrate it into our lives, with wonderful results.

SYNOPSIS

The entire shift toward slowing the pace, gaining focus, simplifying our lives and living in the moment reflects the Spiritual Values of truth and harmony coming into play, as we search for our own truth within. We will seek truth in all that we do including our relationships, the media, and our work and entertainment activities. This will include a pursuit of a simpler lifestyle and a gentler pace, as we increasingly adopt these and other Spiritual Values.

At work, the trend will be toward taking items out of our day. This will allow us to work with greater focus and creativity, as opposed to the multi-tasking approach, which has, until recently, been widely accepted. In the end, we will actually accomplish more through the use of greater creativity in our lives—which is yet another version of the new *less is more* philosophy. Finally, as a byproduct of slowing down to a gentler pace and learning how to let go of outcomes, we will experience less stress and greater enjoyment of life on the whole, which, after all, is the whole point, isn't it!

TRENDS AND IMPLICATIONS

Beginning to Set a New Slower Pace
* We feel the need to balance by slowing down! As a result of slowing down, we will actually feel more productive due to a more creative approach, which will allow us to see solutions more readily.

✳ By paying more attention to those around us, we will become better listeners and therefore better leaders who actually act as harvester of ideas.

Changes to the Media

✳ The networked economy will help us bring news under our control by allowing us to pull to ourselves only the information we need.

✳ We will move to fact-based reports from primary sources and select only categories in which we are interested.

✳ We will find a greater degree of truth in information dissemination in the new age, versus the media version of events in the industrial age of conformity.

✳ News stories will be presented in specially segmented shows that are mostly entertainment based.

From Multi-tasking to Focus

✳ Creativity and focus are proving to be more productive than tackling volumes of work. Taking something out of our day will be an important action. We will move, through various stages, from multi-tasking to a more centered and focused approach to work and life.

✳ More and more people will begin to create time and space for reflection and contemplation as we get off the treadmill of life.

The Simpler Life

✳ We will trend to live in the moment as opposed to placing our attention in the past or the future. Living in the present manifests as contentment.

✳ How we feel about our life will take precedence over money as the motivating factor in our lives in the coming decade.

✳ We will move from social conformity to reinventing our lives on our own terms. The trend is toward scaling back and moving to quieter settings, with simpler homes and furnishings, as people focus on quality over quantity.

✳ The Spiritual value of harmony with one's self and environment will take hold as people find greater joy in life. Simple pleasures such as reading, computer activities, and crafts will become more important

✳ Charitable giving of our time and money will increase as voluntary simplicity allows us to focus more outside of ourselves and make time for others.

Letting Go

✳ We will see greater adoption of the new value: "Let go and enjoy the ride" Half the fun is getting there" will become a truism. With the recognition that the journey is as important as the destination, we will increasingly stop to smell the roses.

✳ The practice of surrendering will gain mainstream acceptance, as more of us discover this brand new concept for attaining personal balance and contentment. We are recognizing that we are not in control; that our inner being has the last word; and that, while we have the responsibility to create our lives, it is best to release our attachment to the outcome.

CHAPTER NINE

Ecology Becomes A Lifestyle

One of the more significant movements today is our society's growing awareness of our interrelationship with the planet we inhabit. The shift in consciousness expressed in our adoption of Spiritual Values is bringing about a greater awareness of our responsibility to take care of not only ourselves, but our home, Earth. And, just as we are learning on a personal level that we get back what we give out, so, as a society, we are now seeing the dramatic effects of this spiritual principle in the ecology of the planet.

Earth Changes: The Planet Reacts

Man has had a great influence on this planet and the results of the industrial age are now visible for all to see and feel. It is no longer necessary for us to rely on scientific data to understand that we will need to change our use of resources and alter our interaction with the planet in order to preserve the same lifestyle for our children. We are all witness to global warming, increases in skin cancer due to the depletion of the ozone layer, extinction of wildlife, and the destruction of arable land from over fertilization and deforestation, to name of few of the planet's current ailments.

As we enter the new millennium, we are beginning to recognize that we have pushed the planet off balance and that the balance will need to be restored—and quickly!

The Heat is On

Our polluting habits and the resultant global warming have set us on a course of earth changes that cause major shifts in radiation and temperature. Global warming is a serious concern as scientists forecast a 6.3 degree temperature rise over the next century. As the temperature rises, we'll feel more than just the heat. The effects are obvious in numerous areas.

In the last year alone, polar warming caused the collapse of 1,150 square miles of ice shelf in the Antarctic. Rising sea levels are killing mangrove forests in Bermuda, and glaciers are melting in India and Peru at a rate of over 100 feet per year. Hurricanes are increasing in frequency in both the Caribbean and southern USA, and forest fires are claiming thousands of square miles of forests in Canada, Indonesia and Spain, to name just a few locations.

In Australia, Korea and California, storms and floods have caused serious damage, and changes to their natural habitat are causing the demise of animals such as the caribou in northern Canada and penguins in Antarctica. In other areas, mosquitoes are moving into non-traditional geography due to weather changes and are spreading disease in Kenya, Columbia and Indonesia.

Earth movements (quakes, volcanic eruptions, etc.) are on the rise at a greater rate than at any other time in the total span of history. But all of these changes make sense when we understand the principle of cause and effect (see chapter 12). How can we expect to detonate nuclear bombs in the Earth without feeling some effects as a result? Every part of the whole is affected by a change in one of the parts. The air temperature, atmospheric composition (pollution), ocean temperature, and plate movements are all linked, in a single finely balanced system. When we introduce a new element to the mix, such as a radical increase in electromagnetic radiation from the new communications installations, the results are sure to affect the whole balance of our world. For instance, we can look for health issues to surface in the new millennium around the increases in electromagnetic radiation (EMR) caused by the escalation of radio wave transmissions from wireless computing and communications devices. All of these are signs of changes to come as the earth reacts to the imbalances we have imposed on it.

We have dramatically altered the balance of nature and the ecosystems of the world and this imbalance has set in motion a chain of events, which is beginning to unfold before our very eyes. These destructive trends are not yet being addressed fast enough and will not be halted, let alone reversed, until drastic action is taken. But what is the likelihood of the major world governments agreeing to significant changes (along with the accompanying economic costs) until a crisis is in full display?

The reaction of the world is only a reflection of our group consciousness or belief system and, sadly, most people today do not address their own health issues by taking early remedial action, such as a change in diet or vitamins. Instead, they wait until they have a full-blown, obvious medical condition before they seek help or take corrective action. By analogy, and historical example, we can deduce that the world will act only when faced with a similar crisis. But we do have a choice. Collectively and as individuals, we can initiate the necessary changes and change ourselves in the process. Or we can wait for the planet to react, as it is doing, so we will be forced to change as a result of drastic planetary changes. Either way, change will come. Of that there is no question.

And Now For the Good News

Fortunately, the new consciousness and our new values are bringing us to a better understanding of our relationship with the planet, each other and the whole of creation. We are beginning to understand what it means to share this planet with the rest of creation, and ecological concern is being expressed by millions of people, with a new sense of care and responsibility for the balance of nature. As individuals, we are looking for greater harmony, not only within ourselves, but in our outer world as well, and our increased ability to respect others is and will continue to be, reflected in an increased respect for nature in all its forms.

Our interest in ecological matters is well developed in a broad range of areas, including land issues such as deforestation, waste management, use of fertilizers and concerns over urban sprawl; animal rights with large scale activism against animal cruelty and numerous causes to save species from extinction; and air and water quality concerns, to mention just a few of the many movements in which people are involved. But this expression is taking on larger social and political proportions in our lives as we integrate ecology into our lifestyles.

In the coming years, we, as a people, will radically alter our view of what ecology means and, as a result, will begin to order our lives around an ecological/frictionless economy, on the one hand, while at the same time being forced to react to earth changes, many of them unpleasant.

The New World will bring about significant change in our

current patterns that will result in a restructuring of our society in great measure. We have already seen the tip of the iceberg emerging with society's reaction to animal testing, ingredients and labeling, pesticide use, and even the exploitation of foreign labor, all of which are simply indications of the wave of change to come. The protection of our natural resources and wildlife, a strong movement today, will soon move beyond the borders of the wetland and the national park and into our neighborhoods and backyards. With the shift into the new millennium, this significant trend of being respectful of nature will continue and, in the later stages of the shift, people will actually feel honored to be visited by nature. More land will be reclaimed for nature and new development projects will get the go ahead only after a full evaluation of potential impact determines the project to be of minimal detriment to nature.

Voluntary Simplicity Becomes a Lifestyle

Ecology as a spiritual principle goes even farther. Spiritually, it means taking into our lives only what we need, living only in the space that we need, and so on. This definition of ecology is about simplicity and economy. It is simplifying our lives. After all, carrying around a lot of possessions can be an unnecessary burden and it requires a lot of energy to store, insure and manage possessions. As we move into the shift, many people are beginning to adopt voluntary simplicity as a conscious lifestyle and to live their lives with just what constitutes enough. There is no sacrifice involved here, however. It is actually a freeing experience to let go, and many in the new millennium will find greater freedom by adjusting their lifestyles with voluntary simplicity in mind.

As more and more people choose this form of living, we will

become increasingly aware of a willingness to let go of the old and will be careful about what new things we bring into our lives. We will look for products that do not use unnecessary packaging and will be more responsible in the disposal of items, recycling wherever possible. This expanded sense of respect and responsibility will extend itself throughout the new-networked economy.

Personal Ecology and the Internet

As we transpose our ecological beliefs from nature to the urban way of life, the new economy will be inherently ecological. This means that the new e-commerce society will evolve as an ecological system, supporting our need for harmony with nature through just-in-time living and more efficient manufacturer-to-consumer systems (the frictionless economy). The resultant delayering of the distribution process will significantly reduce warehousing, transshipping and other intermediary points as the distance between the consumer and manufacturer is collapsed.

The Internet enabled just-in-time economy will also allow us to own only what we need, when we need it. So, as we voluntarily simplify our lives, we will be able to reduce our physical holdings and recycle our unneeded items, thereby using less total world resources. This will be accomplished through time saving, Internet enabled disposal and recycling services operating on a global scale, making it possible for us to easily acquire and divest ourselves of items in a timely fashion.

Towards a New Level of Personal Confidence

Voluntary simplicity is actually about leading an uncluttered life, with greater confidence. As a growing number of people gravitate to simplicity, they will find that they are actually redefining themselves as individuals and they will begin to understand themselves in a unique way.

In the industrial age, to a large extent, we defined ourselves by the way we dressed, the homes and cars we owned and other symbols of financial success. In the new millennium, there will not be the same predominant need to conform as existed in the industrial age consciousness. Today, we see people striving to express their individuality as never before. In the near future, this will lead to a trend of individual expression through our tastes, beliefs, and values in general, rather than through a display of possessions or financial status.

In reality, this movement is a process of letting go of the self as defined by possessions, and a movement toward defining the self in terms of one's true (spiritual) qualities and personal interests. And with this shift comes confidence, the confidence to live life the way we wish to create it, not the way we think others expect us to live. So the shift to ecology involves a change at our very core, as society moves from the ego consciousness, supported by a focus on possessions, to a spiritual-values consciousness, supported by a new self respect and awareness of who we really are as spiritual beings.

Our relationship with the other species on the planet will also be affected as our overall awareness increases. We will begin to recognize that not only are we all equals as human beings, by virtue of our common spiritual heritage, but that all life is precious. By extension, we will begin to understand that, all life is connected as part of the greater whole of creation. Each has its unique part to play—to both give and receive, teach and learn. Everything is interrelated and we all coexist in a finely-balanced relationship. So, as we evolve in the new millennium, we will develop a greater respect for all of creation, animal, vegetable and mineral. This will then affect the way we see and interact with the rest of the world. For example, while the food chain will still be a necessary component of life, the unnecessary killing of animals will fade in popularity. Instead, our decisions and actions will increasingly be motivated and informed by a greater awareness of what constitutes the greater good.

The Planet Will Teach Us About "The Good of the Whole"

The good of the whole will be a dominant spiritual value in the new age. The whole, as stated earlier, is the whole of the universe or creation, and as we come closer to understanding this value, we will move closer to an understanding of our relationship with the Creator.

The Creator provides an equal amount of love to humans, animals, the Earth, and all of the universes. We human beings are loved so much by the Creator that we are allowed to choose our lives and our actions, individually and as a group. In other words, we have been given the freedom that will inevitably teach us both responsibility and service to others, for the greater good.

For some time now, the world has essentially been driven by self-interest and often by greed. In fact, we grew quite self-centered and uncaring as a society over the past 50 years. We loved only ourselves and, in many cases, loved our possessions even more. However, as part of the shift, the new era will be characterized by the opposite qualities of sharing, caring and concern for the good of the whole. Thus, although we will have a great deal of freedom in the new economy, it will ultimately come as a result of giving, which requires one to take attention off of the self.

Values of Sharing and Caring

In the years to come, we will see the values of sharing and caring take hold and contribute to the great shift to a networked society. New levels of communication and services on the Internet will make it easier for us to share our time and our possessions with each other and, in essence, we will develop a new technology-based version of what other sharing communities, such as the Amish, have been doing for over a century. We will learn to support each other and work as a team as we respond to earth crises and solve challenges together. We will learn that we cannot operate alone with the same effectiveness and economy as is gained by working together. And the selfish ego consciousness of the industrial age, characterized by a lack of sharing, will trend into a new spirit of cooperation as we progress into the next century. We will learn to help each other, to give without being asked to do so, and the flow will be toward a genuine caring for one another.

SYNOPSIS

The Earth and its condition are a reflection of our own consciousness. On one hand, the picture might seem rather bleak. The choices we have collectively made with regard to the planet have been abusive and the Earth is reacting. Planetary changes will take on even larger proportions and cause greater imbalances in nature if we progress into the new millennium along the same path we have followed up to now. However, we do have a choice. We can choose to grow by making changes in our lifestyle that move us toward a more harmonious and responsible relationship with the planet and its other inhabitants.

The opportunity exists for us to operate our lives guided by our new awareness of Spiritual Values. The spiritual change in consciousness that comes with the adoption of these new values is changing how we wish to structure and order our lives. We are moving toward a simpler way of being, and this means that we are and will become more aware of what we are taking into our lives and how much we are using. The spiritual gift is that we become more confident in ourselves. Personal contentment will be one major outcome of this new level of confidence.

Of course, we will still have to live out the chain of events we have set in motion, but in doing so we will grow by pulling together and supporting one another. We will find success by working together and we will learn greater truths about love, which is the real reason for our sojourn in this life. Ultimately, we will find the world in the new millennium to be a more sharing, respectful place as we move into a greater harmony with the planet and its inhabitants.

TRENDS AND IMPLICATIONS

New Respect for Nature

* The Planet is reacting to our past collective choices and actions! We are learning that what we give out, we get back. We are beginning to see that everything is connected and interrelated. We will move as a society toward an understanding that when we affect one part of creation, everything else is affected.

* What started as a concern for nature, is now becoming a consciousness that we are applying to everything in our life. Society will restructure around these issues.

* We will develop new levels of respect for all of creation, animal, vegetable and mineral as well as human. This

will dramatically affect our lifestyle and the economy.

✳ Our increasing responsible ecological outlook will lead to higher attention to and concern over product quality, product contents, animal testing, ingredients, pesticide use and even the exploitation of others (foreign labor).

✳ The new Spiritual Values will bring us to the point of taking total responsibility for our lives and our planet.

Voluntary Simplicity

✳ Our sense of self will be defined by our spiritual nature and our true interests and tastes, rather than by our possessions and other people's opinions, so common in the ego-consciousness of the industrial age.

✳ The conscious choice of quality over quantity is on the rise. Quality will be viewed more as an inner, rather than an outer characteristic.

✳ We will more easily let go of the old and be more careful about what we buy and add to our lives. Careful purchasing will also lead to careful disposal. Unnecessary packaging will fall into even greater disfavor.

✳ The frictionless economy will evolve and remove unnecessary intermediaries in the process from manufacturing to delivery of finished goods. The delayering process will reduce both costs and the use of global resources by Western economies.

✳ Just-in-time acquisition and disposal/recycling will work, at both an industry and personal level.

Sharing

✳ A good-of-the-whole consciousness will emerge. E-commerce enabled services will facilitate the development of a greater sense of caring and sharing.

Old models of sharing communities, like the Amish, will be adopted in a virtual form.

✳ New ways of sharing our time and our possessions will reduce demand and save resources. Volunteering and service organizations will grow, as more people discover that giving is truly a rewarding experience.

✳ Helping without having to be asked will become second nature to many. We will learn that freedom is gained by giving to others. A new cooperative spirit will develop.

✳ We will learn more about divine love as we progress toward more harmonious, respectful relationships with ourselves, other people, and the world around us.

CHAPTER TEN

One World:
From Concept To Reality

The move to globalization is nowhere more evident than in the world of business today. Corporations are responding to the needs of the marketplace in order to be more competitive and this is leading to economies of scale on a global basis. Foreign territory is no longer foreign as trade barriers are loosened and cultural styles (seen in global media, entertainment and sports) are adopted and shared around the world. And the acceptance of English as the common language of the Internet and computing is ushering in a new era of communications, which makes the globalization of business just that much easier. All of these changes effect how we view the world we live in and, of course, how we do business.

Freer Trade

Everywhere we look, businesses are stepping across foreign borders to merge, expand or create foreign alliances. The Ford Motor Company now owns Volvo and Jaguar. Sony controls a large part of the motion picture industry. Exxon and Mobil Oil have merged, and national airlines have formed global alliances. A number of banks are considering mergers in Canada, Europe and other areas of the world, to create support structures for their global corporate clients and to better compete on the global stage. Meanwhile, IBM has positioned itself as a global solutions company and Microsoft is likewise a global solutions provider. The needs of such companies and of individuals for global banking will only increase as world commerce and travel expand over the next decade.

We are entering a world of even greater flexibility and freedom, with a networked global economy. The World Trade Organization is slowly unraveling the web of trade restrictions that currently inhibit national growth and competition, and free trade is positioning us for even greater global interaction by facilitating the movement of goods and services, which can be sold in one country and delivered on another continent.

Seeking Personal Freedom to be Global Citizens

As we interact with the whole world, our national boundaries are becoming less important. Spiritually, we are seeking the freedom and ability to create our lives with more flexibility in a global setting. The expansion of e-commerce to a global platform will combine synergistically with this increased desire for freedom and personal responsibility, to propel the world into a global perspective and alter the traditional vision of ourselves as citizens of one country.

The Spiritual Values of harmony, freedom, respect and sharing will be the keys to advancing the world into this new global perspective. As these values are acted upon, in conjunction with the move from a national to a global focus, we will increasingly think of ourselves as citizens of the world. This will be further facilitated by the Internet, which will enable us to create virtual communities, which exist without borders. We will then move away from the traditional anchor points of our nationality or country, migrating instead to identities based on our cultural heritage and personal interests.

Industrial Age Systems are Losing Relevancy

Again, what people are actually seeking is greater control and freedom in their lives, and they want the services in their region, area or neighborhood to reflect this. In other words, people are seeking to create a world of personal expression that responds to their needs.

The large systems of the industrial age are simply no longer serving the individual. As explored in more depth in chapter six, they simply were not designed to serve the individual, and the conformity they imply runs counter to the new movement of personal expression that is manifesting in the business world as "customization for the individual." The new one-to-one marketing approaches are creating new consumer expectations of personalized service levels that specifically address an individual's needs. Today's large systems just are not flexible enough to meet these needs, and they have become bureaucratic and uneconomical as a whole. This runs counter to the new ecological sense of the times.

In the years to come, people will be looking for the framework to express individual creativity in their lives, in their own way. The members of our global society are also seeking, in greater and greater numbers, the freedom to be themselves. So, as we proceed into the new millennium, the large rigid systems will either have to shift, dissolve or transform into a new service model.

Governmental Changes

The drive for freedom and flexibility is reflected in many of the geopolitical changes that have occurred in the last two decades. Some countries have broken into smaller units of governance (USSR, Yugoslavia), while others are facing sovereignty movements (Basques in Spain or Quebecois in Canada). The large units of governance are becoming less important, as we enter the first few years of the shift, for economic and security reasons. On the one hand, we will need and want less government, while, on the other, we desire more relevant governance, as part of the spiritual evolution to an environment which gives us all the opportunity to take full responsibility for our lives. In many cases, smaller units of governance will give us the personal relevance we require in the new global economy.

Changes in government will naturally vary worldwide depending on the spiritual evolution in each area. Overall, however, we will see subtle changes across the board. Already, governments are giving up control (as witnessed with the move toward privatization of the welfare state that began in the 1980s), and national security—once the traditional reason for strong governments—is changing as the world embraces a new value set. This shift will inevitably have implications on our legal, as well as our political, systems.

As Geoff Mulgan, who heads British Prime Minister Tony Blair's policy unit, stated, "This new economy appears to thrive best in particular social environments: ones marked by...light regulation of enterprise, cosmopolitan cultures, and meritocratic openness to women, minorities and outsiders." Societies that are heavily regulated with an abundance of laws rely on the force of law to maintain an orderly society. On the other hand, societies with fewer laws are self-regulated by personal values. As we progress in our adoption of Spiritual Values, we will seek a freer, less-legalized environment, and will instead be guided by our own values. Changes like sunset laws will become popular, as opposed to the current practice of piling laws on the books without a thought given to future reviews of their continuing relevance.

The more control and the tighter the legal framework, the less personal freedom and creativity there will be. But for nations to compete in the new global economy, the creativity of their people will be an important factor in their economic success. Governments will be competing globally for corporate relocations, and countries will have to retain their skilled workers. Taxes in the networked economy will therefore have to be restructured over time to create a level playing field for global business. This will involve shifting the governmental tax base to consumption and away from a reliance on income, which severely limits producers in a global competition for sales, and which governments will have a hard time tracking anyway in a global economy. This shift, along with more efficient and less-costly government services, will assist in plugging the brain drain phenomenon that some countries are experiencing. Conversely, brain-drain may be experienced by countries that do not make such changes.

Borders Change in Function

In the longer time frame, government services will only be needed to provide local services, as we move to this global trading system. Eventually, we will feel no need for borders, as they exist today. The European community is already leading the world in altering the meaning of national borders and is providing greater freedom, while maintaining security from rogue elements in the world. Borders will eventually come to be considered artificial by many of our younger generation by the time they enter the workforce en mass. The views of this new generation will have a significant effect on the meaning of borders and the flow of goods, services and people.

A New Global Morality

The world as a whole is also entering a period of greater stability as the Western alliance extends its values and enforces its vision of what constitutes acceptable behavior in the actions of countries. The obvious example of this was NATO's recent stand in which, for the first time in history, a large part of the Western world formed a police force to control unacceptable behavior in the former Yugoslavia. The NATO alliance action is the first demonstration of the new values being expressed as intervention for the good of the people affected in a given area.

This sense of global morality is also being reflected at national levels, as state of the art communication brings the world to our doorstep, making it harder and harder to keep secrets in this day and age. By and large, our behavior is there for all to see, as our political leaders are discovering. We can all see what is there to be seen, and we can react to whatever we see. The result is a greater sense of morality and accountability on the political stage. This growing sense of morality, on a global scale, is yet another reflection of the mass shift to Spiritual Values.

SYNOPSIS

As the new Spiritual Values consciousness expands, it is ushering in a broad spectrum of changes and a number of themes are converging to yield the reality of One World. At the individual level, a greater desire for freedom, the desire to travel physically and the wish to trade globally via the World Wide Web will reduce our need for borders and barriers as they exist today. The drive for more personal responsibility is also reducing the need for government services. The services we do require will be economically delivered to meet our individual needs. Smaller units of governance will give us the personal relevance we require in the new global economy, and the new consciousness represented by our new Spiritual Values will continue to be reflected in the actions of our governments, with the result seen in continued world stability.

TRENDS AND IMPLICATIONS

The New Global Citizen

* Free trade is positioning us for greater global interaction.
* Millions will bank their money in different lands and invest internationally.
* The Internet will enable us to create virtual communities, without need of borders. As we move from a national focus to global, we will shift our anchor points to our cultural roots and/or our personal interest groups, and identify less with our nationality.
* Public need for greater freedom and control has led to privatization movements.
* We will shift to thinking of ourselves as global citizens. Many people will live in several countries. World Travel

will expand enormously. Intermarriage between different cultures will increase as communication expands.

Governments and Borders

✳ The large systems and institutions of the industrial age will shift, dissolve, or transform to better serve the individual.

✳ Governments will need to create a level playing field in the global economy. Jurisdictions will compete globally for new corporate locations, with competitive taxes and incentives.

✳ Countries will need to retain skilled workers. The brain drain experienced by some countries will be plugged with a shift to consumption taxes and overall more efficient, less costly government services. Conversely, brain-drain will be experienced by countries that do not make such changes.

✳ E-commerce will lead to less importance being placed on national borders as control points for goods and services.

Global Standards

✳ A new global morality is here as the shift to Spiritual Values spreads from Western society to many other countries. NATO's reaction to curb unacceptable behavior in Yugoslavia is a key example.

✳ Global news and other electronic media are creating a new openness of information. Ethics are standardizing globally due to electronic information distribution. No one (including leaders and government) can hide unacceptable behavior.

✳ WTO, ISO, European Monetary Union and global entertainment point the way to global integration.

CHAPTER ELEVEN

Spiritual Economics: The Redefinition Of Wealth

One of the biggest changes to occur in the next decade, and one that is implicit in all of the trends and changes discussed in the preceding chapters, is the shift to a new understanding and belief about the nature of wealth. In fact, the emergence of a new definition of wealth is a major component of the millennium shift and the widespread adoption of Spiritual Values. As our values change and we gain a greater understanding of who we are as spiritual beings, we are beginning to see wealth in new and different ways, and what was once a goal in its own right is no longer the end point of our endeavors. Instead, we are seeking the qualities which money can bring into our lives and the lives of others.

All of this, of course, affects the way that we view wealth and money, and will ultimately affect the economy as a whole, as we gradually shift to an economy that is driven by our new Spiritual Values. It therefore behooves us, as leaders and entrepreneurs, to know how to work with these new concepts and values. As I began to identify the key trends that are reshaping our world and to see how the new values are at play in these changes, I distilled my observations into a new discipline called Spiritual Economics, which allows us to do just that. Spiritual Economics is all about working with the new values to create a redefined wealth for ourselves, our corporations and even our nations.

A New Definition of Wealth

The traditional concept of wealth has been the accumulation of money or physical assets such as land, jewels, gold, businesses, and the like. But we hear all the time about people dying and leaving behind vast sums of money, yet having lived in very simple, and sometimes dire, circumstances during their lives. This begs the question, "What is the point of working long hard days, earning large sums of money, only to die and pass it on to family or the government, without ever having enjoyed it ourselves?" Most of us would be hard pressed to see the merit of such an arrangement, yet this is how many people conducted their lives in the industrial age.

Today, however, the understanding of wealth and the search for it is in transition to a new level. What is emerging is a trend of expressing and enjoying our lives as we go, living in the moment as opposed to postponing our joy to some future time when we will finally have the time and/or the money we think we need. As many of us understand, that future point in time never arrives, because when we finally get enough money, we no longer have the capacity to live a changed life anyway. We simply would not be able to change a lifetime habit of accumulating wealth and make a 180 degree turn to become a giver and liver of life. And so, we are increasingly seeking to enjoy life as we live it, to enjoy the people we love and the activities we want to do, and to do so not as some dream delayed, but right now, this moment. In doing this, we actually redefine and claim real wealth in our lives.

The New Search for Quality of Life

What we are seeing is a new understanding of wealth, which encompasses our personal growth and how we feel about our lives. This is a big step from hoping life will be beautiful once we have achieved our financial goals or have the money we are working so hard to acquire. At the same time, we are learning that money does not guarantee happiness, and so the shift is about changing our focus to the real goal, which is quality of life and how we feel.

The new definition of wealth that is emerging expands on currency and monetary definitions, and includes a concept of quality of life which implies much more than our material circumstances. It entails the qualities that our acquisitions facilitate. For instance, we want joy in our lives. We want to feel contentment, to see beauty, and have the freedom to enjoy all that life has to offer. In other words, we are seeking the qualities that wealth brings us, the way that it enriches our lives and the lives of others, rather than the physical thing itself. Having these qualities in our lives makes us truly wealthy.

This shift in the definition of wealth is at the root of the greatest change mankind will make in its history. And the shift has already begun. We are actually migrating to a higher view by redefining wealth, not as something that is accumulated, but as something to be enjoyed and shared. In making this shift, we begin looking for ways to use our physical assets to benefit ourselves and the world. And, by giving of ourselves in this way, we ultimately receive much more than money. We receive and attract new qualities into our life. These new qualities are spiritual in nature and bring true quality to our life.

The True Meaning of Currency

The shift to viewing wealth as something to be shared is another significant trend that accompanies this redefinition of wealth. We are actually beginning to work with the spiritual principle of giving, which is described in Chapter 12. In the process, we are learning how to give, and we are learning that by giving we also receive. What this means, when it comes to money, is that it is more productive to keep the flow or the current (currency) moving, in order to receive. This shift brings with it a new understanding of money that allows us to grasp the true meaning of currency.

In all things there is an inflow and outflow. In life, we as individuals are constantly receiving but if we do not pass it on, we are stopping or bottlenecking the flow. Thus, to keep money in circulation is to keep it flowing. This creates the currency so many of us desire.

Essentially, we attract into our lives that which we give out. When we give love, we receive it and to receive it we must give it. The same is true for other Spiritual qualities we wish to have such as harmony, good cheer, and respect. And the same holds true for wealth. This concept is both a reflection of the Spiritual Values we are adopting on a broad scale and is a major component of Spiritual Economics.

Spiritual Economics: A New Way of Living and Working

Traditional economics is the science of the production and distribution of material wealth. Spiritual Economics has the same outcome—wealth. However, the gaining of wealth from a spiritual perspective encompasses both currency and the Spiritual Values that often accompany it such as freedom, contentment, joy, giving and at least a dozen other qualities.

I define Spiritual Economics as the ongoing search for, discovery and application of Spiritual Principles (such as respect, love, giving, compassion, etc.) to one's work, play and relationships. This brings new spiritual qualities into one's life (such as joy, freedom, self-assurance etc.) as well as the qualities inherent in material wealth.

This is the way we grow. We apply what we have learned spiritually to our everyday life, acting as a positive example for all whom we meet. To work with Spiritual Economics is to work in harmony with all life and the planet, knowing that everything is a connected part of the whole. One begins to think of oneself as an integral part of the whole a well. Such a person works for the good of the whole and is defined as wholistic.

A key aspect of the practice of Spiritual Economics is the understanding that one is on a journey of discovery. As a result, one recognizes that the practice of Spiritual Economics itself is constantly unfolding. It is a creative process, not a static one, and it involves constant evolution and creativity in the discovery of the deeper meaning of Spiritual concepts and their application to the challenges in our life, whether at home, work or play.

Working with Spiritual Economics will be highly profitable, as it is proven in the practice of working with a higher set of laws, universal laws or principles which are more fully defined in the next chapter. First, one becomes aware that these keys to life exist and then one begins to apply them to his or her own life and way of interacting with others. Finally, one carries these values out into the working world as they seek new ways to incorporate Spiritual Principles into organizations. The effect of operating from the viewpoint of a higher self, a spiritual self, results in a set of personal operating behaviors that are defined as Spiritual Values. By working with these new values, and understanding how they inform and influence the trends, we can actually lead the market and profit via the new wealth.

SYNOPSIS

As part of our shift to a greater understanding of who we are as spiritual beings, we are literally redefining our concepts of wealth and quality of life to mean far more than material abundance and the standard of living. This shift is both the result of and is fueling the millennium shift and our increasing adoption of Spiritual Values, as we move toward a networked economy. My observation of this shift, with its attendant trends and changes, has given rise to the new discipline of Spiritual Economics.

The practice of Spiritual Economics entails the application of Spiritual Principles to every aspect of one's life, and manifests as personal qualities that can be described as Spiritual Values. It incorporates the new definition and understanding of wealth with our increasing adoption of Spiritual Values, so that we can actually work with Spiritual Principles to manifest abundance in our lives in a way that is aligned with the highest. But the real key lies in understanding and working with certain key Spiritual Principles which inform and indeed are the basis of the new Spiritual Values we are adopting.

TRENDS AND IMPLICATIONS

* Wealth is now being redefined in terms of how we feel, not what we have.
* We are looking for quality of life, not just quantity. And quality is being defined in terms of Spiritual Values.
* We will give more freely of our time and money as we begin to understand the true nature of currency and the principle of giving.

CHAPTER TWELVE

Understanding the New Spiritual Values

Five Underlying Principles

The Spiritual Values that have been referenced throughout the previous chapters are derived from and based upon Universal/Spiritual Principles. At their core, these Spiritual Principles and the Spiritual Values they foster are based on a body of very old wisdom found in many writings throughout the ages. When we understand the deeper meaning of these Spiritual Principles and align our behavior with them, we will be in harmony with the universe around us. In fact, one definition of consciousness is our degree of understanding of Universal /Spiritual Principles and their incorporation into how we live our lives. These principles serve a valuable purpose in helping us to know how to behave in the context of our life experiences. By consciously working with them, we can be guided in making the shift to operating smoothly in the new global consciousness.

The increasing adoption of Spiritual Values in the workplace, business sector and our personal lives is a starting place for understanding the Universal/Spiritual Principles explored in this chapter. For your reference, a partial list of these Spiritual Values is provided on the following page.

Spiritual Values

Honesty	Forgiveness	Humor
Love	Detachment	Contentment
Right Discrimination	Humility	Joy
Enthusiasm	Sharing	Respect
Flexibility	Trust	Harmony
Listening	Caring	Empathy
Grace	Charity	Discipline
Order	Purity	Kindness
Freedom	Openness	Truthfulness
Acceptance	Gratitude	Thankfulness
Openness	Helpfulness	Cheerfulness
Compassion	Responsibility	Tolerance

Millions of people are beginning to express their lives around these new values and so they are an important point of focus for those who wish to orient their lives around these positive behaviors and live in harmony with the Spiritual Principles, which actually guide the new value set.

I have selected five Spiritual Principles which are at the root of these Spiritual Values, but there are many more. These principles can show us how the universe works and how we, as spiritual beings, interact with the universe or the Creator. But they require contemplation and study to grasp their full meaning. Just as there is always one more step in our growth in the journey of Soul, as discussed in the introduction, there is always one more step to be taken in our understanding of the Spiritual Principles that guide us on our journey. The Spiritual Principles offered in this chapter are a starting point for you. It is my hope that this book and the principles explored in the following pages will assist you in your journey.

The Principle of Economy

The Principle of Economy relates to the best use of resources to achieve a given result. In the context of this discussion on the adoption of Spiritual Values and the technological transformation of our society, this Principle encompasses two major themes:

- it provides us with guidance on the management and use of the earth's resources
- it offers us a template for working towards our spiritual goals.

Current ecological movements and the growing acceptance of the concept of voluntary simplicity both reflect the operation of the first theme. In this context, the Principle of Economy means using only what we need and no more. It is about keeping in our lives only those things that we can reasonably use and implies a cleaner, uncluttered personal environment, in which we can move and live without unnecessary baggage. Divesting ourselves of unnecessary things in this way can be a very freeing exercise, but it also involves being careful about what we continue to acquire.

The economy of the 1980's was characterized by consumerism and the purchasing of goods, often purely for the pleasure of making the purchase. Many times, items bought impulsively were used once and then discarded or left to gather dust in a closet. In contrast, we are seeing the beginnings of a shift to careful acquisition, with a recognition of the value of quality. This shift is behind the current resurgence in the appeal of brand names and the quality they represent. This trend in the direction of careful purchasing of necessary quality items will expand in the new economy.

The whole concept of owning less, but choosing quality and durability in what we do purchase, is both ecological and economical. The use of the term economy in this context of the Principle again means being economical with the Earth's resources. Recycling and reusing are part of the equation, as is the trend toward a sharing culture, as demonstrated in communities like the Amish, the Mennonite and other groups, who operate by sharing common tools and equipment. These groups provide an example of the kind of sharing and sense of community we will have an opportunity to form as part of the shift to a new values set in the new century.

This principle can also be applied to the economy as a whole. The term "frictionless economy" implies less waste and a greater ease of interaction. In the frictionless economy, which is now emerging and will take firm hold in the networked economy of the new century, the distance between buyer and manufacturer is narrowing. This is due to the elimination of middlemen and distribution layers which are both unnecessary and uneconomical.

The second major aspect of the Principle of Economy deals with an economical or direct approach to our spiritual growth. It refers to taking the path of least resistance and assuming complete responsibility for our journey. This doesn't necessarily mean taking the easy road. It means going with the flow, following our heart, and doing what we feel is right for us. This applies to our choices of residence, work, relationships, and all other decisions that lead us to a different life focus.

In yet another sense, the Principle of Economy refers to another important principle, reminding us that as we move along in life, we must pay for everything we get. There is no free ride and, sooner or later, we must make our own way. Everything we receive should be earned in some way, either by paying for it, working for it, by trade or by receiving it as a gift. By receiving money we have not earned, we simply invite the scales of Spiritual justice (Karma) to correct this imbalance. The scales of Spiritual justice are exacting and any dishonesty will eventually return to us, as a lesson for our growth. It therefore behooves us to pursue the most direct path toward our spiritual goals by simply ensuring that the scales are equal and that we have paid for everything we receive.

In the new millennium will also learn that the pursuit of money for its own sake is often out of touch with our wish to follow our heart's desires. As society adopts and reorients around Spiritual Values, we will begin to focus on others and take attention away from self. This shift includes a movement from a self-driven world to a service-to-others world, which will open our hearts to new possibilities. These possibilities already show signs of taking hold as more and more people seek a slower paced environment with a sense of genuine community. Some call this cashing out, but it is really a reflection of the new Spiritual Values. What becomes important is time with the family, as opposed to briefly scheduled intervals of quality time, and the ongoing overall quality of life.

In this context, the Principle of Economy instructs us on the necessity of slowing down, taking time for ourselves, actually learning to love ourselves and then passing that love on to others in our life. This offers us the best and most direct opportunity to grow in our relationship with our inner self, with nature, and with the Creator. This is the essence of the Principle of Economy. It is about taking the most direct and economical path, the road with the least friction in our personal discovery of our true essence as Soul.

The Principle of Reversed Effort

The Principle of Reversed Effort is in part about letting go and slowing down. In today's world, where everything is speeding up, both of these actions can appear contrary to the requirements of success. To many of us, it seems logical that we must work longer, harder, and faster, and push with all our strength to achieve our goals. Our upbringing has taught us to push hard for what we want and, if we do not get it, to push even harder. In reality, however, the harder we struggle to achieve something, the more difficult it becomes. The Principle of Reversed Effort allows us to begin to understand this concept and to abandon force as a means of achieving our goals. In practical terms, this means not forcing outcomes and results, and learning to work smarter rather than harder.

As the pace of change increases and many of us are faced with information overload, the idea of slowing down can seem particularly contrary to us. Yet this is exactly what we must do to survive. Slowing down is the only way we can get in touch with our true selves and begin to access higher degrees of insight, awareness and creativity, which will allow us to adapt, survive and succeed in a rapidly changing world. It is an example of a reversed effort. If we continue to pound our feet on the treadmill of life, we will just go round and round repeating experiences until we eventually wonder what life is all about. At that point one is usually ready for something new. Old habits, patterns and mental concepts of what is right and wrong are hard to change, but the Principle of Reversed Effort can help us understand that we do not have to feel guilty about slowing down. In fact, by slowing our pace we can actually become more productive than we can currently imagine.

When we apply this Principle to our lives, we see that the

process of slowing down to a saner pace allows us to see more clearly, gain insight and develop more creative solutions. This is crucial, since life is about solving problems as we progress on the journey. The manner in which we handle our challenges constitutes the prime mechanism Soul employs to gain experience and grow. Moving at a slower pace establishes a calmer personal environment, which better enables us to find creative, intelligent solutions. And life becomes much more enjoyable when we slow down, smell the roses, and spend more time with our families and friends.

Letting go of outcomes is another major theme of the Principle of Reversed Effort. As discussed, in the industrial age, we grew up learning to push for what we want. Most of us, however, have not learned how to move with the flow. We spend our lives pushing hard to achieve our objectives, often without success. As we continue to do what we have been taught and simply push harder when the going gets tough, this can lead to frustration and anger.

The Principle of Reversed Effort teaches us that when we find ourselves facing resistance, we need to understand that we are moving against the flow. We are all connected (see the Principle of Harmony) and there are millions of points at which our personal agendas connect with those of others, of nature and the universe. It may be that there is a better way to go about achieving our goal, which would likewise be better for the whole. The key to understanding this Principle is knowing that not all things are meant to be the way we have mentally formulated them and wish them to manifest.

The secret of this Principle rests in learning to let go of outcomes. This means that while it is good to have and to work toward our goals, we need to let the universe take care of exactly how they manifest. We all want a certain outcome for our plans but there is a higher order of things and we need to be aware of this fact. In order to move in harmony with that higher order, we need to stop pushing so hard for our desired end and let the universe deliver it to us in the manner that is best for all concerned. An expression sums up this Principle: "Not my will, but Thy will be done." In other words the Creator knows what to do. We don't have to give It specific instructions.

By turning our expectations over to the universe (or the Creator) and assuming a state of detachment from our desires and wishes for a particular outcome, we open ourselves to the creative input from other people, our inner self, and the universe around us. The Principle of Reversed Effort teaches us to do all that we can to set our creativity in motion, and then to relax and let the universe provide. Learning to act in this manner can be very rewarding as well as relieving, as we learn to relax and stop worrying about outcomes that we cannot control.

The Principle of Giving

As we enter the new age, we are changing our values and our focus is shifting from self-centered living to a new sharing, based on the recognition that we are all connected. We are beginning to understand that when we affect one part of an ecosystem or an environment, we affect our personal world, too. Similarly, when we affect another person, we affect ourselves, since we are all part of the whole. As the new Spiritual Values become a way of being for many, our interest in giving to others is also growing.

The Principle of Giving is at the root of this shift to a sharing consciousness. When we share of ourselves we are actually living examples of Spiritual Values and, as a result, we gain in our understanding of the underlying Spiritual Principles. We begin to recognize that each person must make their own way and become responsible for their own life, but we are also prepared to help when help is needed. Thus, where we were once focused inwardly on our own wants and desires, we are now turning outward and seeing the benefits of giving.

Placing an undue amount of attention on the self is actually at the root of many diseases, such as depression, in today's society. But the inward focus on the self, which can be described as a negative downward spiral, can be reversed with a giving heart, by placing our attention on helping others. The sense of giving and willingness to share can manifest as a newly found joy and contentment in our lives, and a feeling that we are doing exactly what we were meant to do in life. This is no surprise since our main purpose as Soul, is to learn how to love.

We can all move to create a positive joyful life by giving. A good way to start is by finding one kind deed to do each day. It may take the form of a compliment, a kind word, or an expression of caring or love, but it must be done without thought of reward or acknowledgement. One of the best ways to give is through a silent act of service. Giving in this manner is a sure way to open the heart and bring love into one's life, for, when we give of ourselves in this way, without thought of recognition or compensation, we are giving from the heart. This form of giving is true service to the whole. When we serve one of the creator's other beings in this way, we are actually serving the creator, which opens us up even more to the creator's love for all life.

The creator loves everything in its creation with an equal amount of love. It allows each being or Soul to grow and learn at it's own pace and in its own way. In fact, it has created this entire process of learning in such a way as to give us complete freedom to make our own choices and to learn from those choices. Eventually we learn that we get back just what we give out. To treat our fellow beings and all of creation with respect—in the knowledge that each of us is making our own way on the journey home to the center of creation—is to give love in the truest sense. This is Spiritual or Divine Love. It means not interfering in the growth and the lessons of another, but giving service to others if they would like help, in a selfless or silent fashion.

Giving service to others is a significant way to open the heart to love. Opening the heart means developing an empathy for others and recognizing that, while we cannot alter the circumstances of their lives (which they require in order to learn their own spiritual lessons), we can show compassion. The Spiritual gifts of life flow back to us, often in subtle yet substantial ways, when we learn to integrate giving from the heart into our lifestyle, and we learn more about true Spiritual or Divine Love.

The Principle of Harmony

Scientists now acknowledge that the universe, in all its forms, is comprised of energy. The entire universe consists of a broad spectrum of energy, some of it invisible to us and beyond the human mind's ability to comprehend. Even we, as human beings are, of this energy. In its ultimate simplicity, this energy is Light and Sound. These two common factors bind together everything in the universe, and everything is vibrating at a specific rate which determines its form, color, sound, smell, etc. This energy is also interactive and when one thing changes, it changes the whole and all of its parts. *The Principle of Harmony* is therefore about working in harmony with the whole of life. Indeed, the very word, harmony, implies the element of sound, thus harmonics. The opposite, of course, is discord.

When we work in harmony with nature, we do not disturb the energy of the system in which we are interacting. Likewise, when we work in harmony with each other, we are operating together like a finely tuned machine. When companies have internal conflict, they waste time and energy fighting each other instead of cooperating in the production of a better, more competitive product. And on the other hand, when we clear-cut forests we create an imbalance in nature, the result of which is erosion and flooding. When we understand that we are all creating an effect on each other and our world, we can begin to be a force for cooperation, peace, respect, and dozens of other Spiritual Values.

The Principle of Harmony is about becoming aware of our interrelationship with each other, our world, the universe and every aspect of its makeup. It is also about recognizing our existence as spiritual beings and understanding that our consciousness is related to our rate of vibration. In fact, these two concepts are linked.

Our awareness of the Principle of Harmony is an ever-expanding process in which there is always one more step to take in our unfoldment.

The Principle of Love

The concept of love that most people hold is a romantic one, but there is a much deeper meaning of love, from a spiritual perspective. Here I am referring to the Spiritual or Divine Love that starts with the creator. We Souls were created out of this love and were set upon our journey to gain deeper and deeper understandings of what that love is all about. The creator is considered the center of love, and our journey is about returning to that center of our own accord, through our personal experiences.

Each of us is on our own unique version of this journey and our lessons are custom designed for us. The creator has given us complete freedom in this journey to make our own choices and to learn personal responsibility from our experiences and mistakes. In other words, we have the freedom to grow in our own unique way and in our own time. Thus, what might appear easy to one person could be extremely difficult for another, based on the lessons that Soul is working on. The creator, however, has an unlimited amount of love for all of us, which does not wane, regardless of what we might do, say or think. This is the foundation of the Principle of Love.

The Principle of Love here on earth operates on the same basis and is all about giving other Souls the space they need to grow. When we truly love another, we accept them the way they are, without wanting to change them. We give them the space and freedom they need to create their world, without our interference, which includes unsolicited advice. If we interfere with the lessons of another, we are limiting their ability to grow because they can only learn from their own personal experience. Love means respecting each Soul and its need to learn in its own way. The cost for unwanted interference is that we can sometimes pick up some of the difficulties involved in the other person's lesson. This is referred to as taking on the Karma of another. Most of us have enough lessons of our own to work on, without taking on someone else's!

It is also important to understand that we can actually invade another person's space in the course of wanting to help them. To avoid any unintended and unwanted intrusion into the space of another person, it is always best to ask if the person would like to hear what we have to say before we offer advice, and to ask if they would like our help, before giving it. Of course, there are some exemptions. For instance, when we are young we need both guidance and love from our parents. And certainly, if another person was in danger, we would immediately do all we could to help. When we do have time to ask, however, it is best to offer help and provide it only when permission has been given.

In this way, we learn to give others the respect we would like for ourselves in our own journey. We are then better able to grant to all Souls the unconditional acceptance that is the basis of the Principle of Love.

A New Beginning

As defined in the foregoing pages there are numerous trends being fueled by the adoption of spiritual values in Western society. At present, a minority in society is driving these trends. However, there is a genuine opportunity for our society to change en mass. This change starts with the individual; you and me. As leaders we have a great opportunity to be pioneers in the context of spiritual history. We can begin to consciously live our lives filled with spiritual values and in this way we will truly change our personal world and the world at large.

As I have alluded to in the first chapter, we will only be able to take full advantage of the new technologies if we are spiritually ready. We will need to change as a whole society to accept the gifts that we are receiving and that are about to manifest. In other words, the significant social benefits of the shift to the new technologically driven society will only fully come about with our adoption of a new spiritually motivated set of values. For example, as freedom gained is a function of responsibility accepted, so the responsible use of the Internet will give us new degrees of freedom. Conversely, the corruption of the use of the Internet which is motivated by selfish gain or by others that invade the privacy of the individual, will slow the growth and benefits that this technology can bring. The same is true for microchip card technology that has the ability to simplify our lives and provide many with a new degree of freedom, but, if misused, also has the power to cause an invasion of privacy through the misuse of personal data, or the monitoring of personal movements.

In the first chapter, The Millennium Shift, I described the third transition of man that we are living through today. As part of this transition, the human race has a choice, as reflected in what we do as individuals, and that choice is to move beyond the self and to reach out to others, and to live and act in harmony with all of creation. The new technological age has the potential to create sufficient wealth and time necessary to enable a large segment of society to go deeper into the search and to discover who they are and why they are here. This search is about discovering our true identity; a spiritual being called Soul. And this discovery will open up a whole different value set founded upon Spiritual Values.

We will be able to create the time in our lives to do this, but only if we are prepared to change. This is why I dedicated a whole chapter to the action and benefits of slowing down. The ability to accept and adapt in a responsible, ethical manner to the new technology centers on this change. Just as the industrial age gave us the ability and time to create and express our lives in the form of art, literature, music, dance, sculpture etc., the new age will give us the ability to create richer more meaningful lives with new spiritual awareness. And we will do this by discovering who we really are and who we can become as spiritual beings having a human life.

We all have the power to create our lives in our own way, and how we do this affects the whole that we are all part of.

What we give out to others is what we are!

G. Robert Switzer

Business Visionary ~ Speaker ~ Futurist

For more than twenty years, G. Robert Switzer has been leading corporations in planning for the future. He has worked in the repositioning of business, non-profit, and governmental organizations such as American Express, YMCA and Public Television, to focus on the needs of customers. Much of his leadership has involved the design of new products and services, and the formation of strategic alliances to bring unique value and service levels to market.

Mr. Switzer has spent over ten years consulting to corporations in the design and development of customer loyalty and value-added programs. In his most recent corporate position as General Manager, New Ventures, for a leading retailer, he has worked with the latest technologies to create new customer focused services.

He is an accomplished corporate presenter and, for over fifteen years, has conducted numerous workshops on Spiritual topics such as "The Spiritual Meaning of Dreams," "The Journey of Soul", and "How to Master Change From A Spiritual

Perspective." And in numerous talks on a broad range of spiritual topics, he has helped others gain insights and find new ways to be successful, solve problems, and bring joy into their lives by increasing their understanding of their spiritual mission and discovering their own unique relationship with creation.

Mr. Switzer explored many spiritual disciplines, teachings and healing therapies and, through the practice of daily spiritual exercises that he has learned, has uncovered numerous spiritual insights, which he now shares in his work.

As a futurist and visionary, Mr. Switzer combines his strategic business knowledge with Spiritual awareness in offering this unique view of present trends and their likely future implications.

Let's Communicate

I welcome your comments and observations with respect to the sharing of universal truths, as well as the forces of change and their likely outcomes as explored in this work.

Would you like to share your vision for the future?

What trends can you see emerging?

Would you like to share how you have fostered Spiritual Values in your life, in your corporation, or with family and friends?

Do you have questions/issues you would like me to address in future writings?

What did you like about this book?
How can I improve it for subsequent printings?

Please feel free to email to me your thoughts and questions at:

www.trendzbook.com